FOR SALE BY OWNER
KIT

Fourth Edition

Robert Irwin

Dearborn™
Trade Publishing
A **Kaplan Professional** Company

This publication is designed to provide accurate and authoritative information in regard to the subject matter covered. It is sold with the understanding that the publisher is not engaged in rendering legal, accounting, or other professional service. If legal advice or other expert assistance is required, the services of a competent professional person should be sought.

Acquisitions Editor: Mary B. Good
Senior Managing Editor: Jack Kiburz
Cover Design: KTK Design Associates
Interior Design: Lucy Jenkins
Typesetting: Elizabeth Pitts

Published by Dearborn Trade Publishing, a Kaplan Professional Company

Printed in the United States of America

02 03 04 10 9 8 7 6 5 4 3 2 1

Library of Congress Cataloging-in-Publication Data

Irwin, Robert, 1941-
  The for sale by owner kit / Robert Irwin.— 4th ed.
     p.   cm.
Includes index.
  ISBN 0-7931-5026-4
1. House selling—Handbooks, manuals, etc. 2. House selling—United
States—Handbooks, manuals, etc.   I. Title.
  HD1379 .I644 2002
  333.33′8—dc21
                                                    2001007521

Contents

How to Sell Your Home Quickly

How much are you willing to pay an agent to help sell your home?

Will you pay 6 percent, a "full" commission?

What about 4 percent, a "discounted" commission?

Maybe you'll pop for 3 percent, a "buyer's agent" commission.

Or perhaps you don't want to pay more than 1 percent, an "assisted sale" commission.

Then again, maybe you're a purist and don't want to pay anyone else a dime—a true sale by owner.

Today, you have your choice, from paying a full commission to none at all. And however you choose, you still stand a good chance of getting your home sold. (One national organization predicted that by 2010 nearly 40 percent of *all* home sales in the United States would be FSBO, or for sale by owner, in one form or another.)

Why Would You Want to Sell FSBO?

For most people, the answer is easy: to save money. Take a look at the amount of commission typically charged in a sale at various price points. (Note: There is no "standard" commission; agents can charge whatever they want. But the typical full-service commission nationwide is around 6 percent.)

Sales Price	Rate	Commission
$ 100,000	6%	$ 6,000
125,000	6	7,500
150,000	6	9,000
175,000	6	10,500
200,000	6	12,000
225,000	6	13,500
250,000	6	15,000
275,000	6	16,500
300,000	6	18,000
350,000	6	21,000
400,000	6	24,000
450,000	6	27,000
500,000	6	30,000
550,000	6	33,000
600,000	6	36,000
700,000	6	42,000
800,000	6	48,000
900,000	6	54,000
1,000,000	6	60,000

As you can see, for even a modest home of $100,000 the commission is still a hefty $6,000. But by the time the price gets to $500,000, that 6 percent is up to $30,000. For most people, that's serious money.

The Big Objections to Big Commissions

To many people, the commissions seem out of proportion. There are at least three reasons for this.

1. No relation to equity. It doesn't matter if your equity is 100 percent of the home's sale price or 10 percent, the commission is the same.

For example, suppose that you are selling a home for $200,000, and you have equity in it of 10 percent (which is not all that uncommon). That means, in reality, you own $20,000 of the home and the lender owns $180,000. If you list your home at 6 percent, your commission cost would be $12,000. Expressed as a percentage of equity, the commission would be 60 percent! That's right, you would end up paying more than half of what you owned in the property in the commission (and most of the rest would go for closing costs!).

Of course, many people have a much larger equity. Nevertheless, in the past, there has been debate in real estate circles as to how to structure a commission in relationship to what the seller truly owns in the home and not by the sales price. Indeed, a few companies have tried equity-based commissions in the past. Unfortunately, none has been widely successful.

2. Poorly defined relationship to price. Many sellers of higher-priced homes have asked the question, Is it really that much harder to sell higher-priced properties than less expensive homes? For example, the seller of a $100,000 home at 6 percent pays $6,000 in commission. The seller of a million-dollar home at 6 percent pays $60,000, ten times as much. The question then becomes, Is it really ten times more difficult or ten times more work to sell the more expensive property?

Many agents argue that given the egos of some of the people who own million-dollar homes, it is ten times more difficult! Seriously, however, it is a valid question. After all, the process is usually identical and the paperwork similar.

In response, many real estate companies are turning to a fixed fee-for-service policy, which is sort of like going to the doctor. There's one fee for an appendicitis, another for an endoscopic exam, and yet another for evaluating a sore throat. Presumably, the doctor doesn't charge a percentage of the total medical costs but rather has a fee for each service. A new wave of real estate agents is doing the same thing.

Thus, there may be a fee of, say, $750 for filling out a sales agreement, $500 for handling disclosures, $250 for the escrow agreements, and so forth. Chapter 4 is devoted to fee-for-service brokers.

3. The commission rate is set too high. Most sellers resent the idea of paying 6 percent of their sales price to an agent. Those who have long memories recall that "in the old days" when homes sold for $20,000 (the *very* old days!), the typical commission rate was only 5 percent. That meant that agents only got $1,000 for their efforts. Now, with prices ten times higher, agents get an additional 1 percent.

Further, on the East Coast, there are real estate lawyers who regularly handle the paperwork for the sellers in a transaction, and their typical fee is between $500 and $1,500, even today. The argument goes, Why should agents charge so much when even lawyers charge so little?

In response, discount brokers have popped up all over the country. They offer much reduced commissions, typically 1 percent to the seller (although if a buyer's agent is involved, the commission can be as much as a total of 4 percent). See Chapter 5 for more about discount brokers.

Choices Abound

If you don't want to pay a full commission to an agent to sell your home, you're in good company. I suspect most sellers feel exactly the same way.

And as noted above, today you have many good alternatives. However, only a short time ago, you had just two choices: a full commission or none at all. There were few agents who would work for less than the full amount, which meant that a FSBO seller had to go it entirely alone, a sometimes daunting task.

Is There Really a Lot of Work in Selling a Home?

This brings us to the other side of the coin. Thus far, we've been talking exclusively about what an agent makes when he or she sells your home. However, as any good agent will tell you, there's always work involved in the sale of a property, sometimes a great deal of work.

At this point, many people, especially those who have never sold a home on their own, are apt to jump in with the observation that there isn't really much work involved. After all, it wasn't that long ago when there was a huge nationwide seller's market—homes were selling within days of being put on the market, sometimes within hours! Sometimes for more than the asking price!

Yes, it's true that in a seller's market a big part of the selling process, namely the part involved in finding a buyer, becomes easy. It wasn't that long ago that buyers were knocking on doors trying to find willing sellers.

Finding a buyer, however, is not the same as closing a deal. Even with a buyer in hand, there is still work required to close the sale, as shown in Figure 1.1.

Remember, all of the above work must be done *after* you've found your buyer. If you also need to hook a buyer, you can count on a whole lot more.

Who Does the Work?

If you pay a full-commission agent, he or she does all the work. But if you don't pay a full commission, you can't expect the agent to do all that work. Yet, it's still there. It still needs to be done. So who's going to do it?

Yes, the correct answer is you.

Pay an agent a full commission to handle the sale for you, then presumably the agent is going to do all of the heavy lifting. On the other hand, if you pay less than a full commission, some of that burden shifts to you. The less you pay, the more of the burden you must shoulder all the way down to where you pay nothing, as a FSBO, and have to do *all* of the work yourself.

FIGURE 1.1

Work Required to Close a Sale after You Find the Buyer

- Qualifying the buyers (to be sure they can afford your home).
- Completing a binding sales agreement (to be sure you do, indeed, have a legitimate sale).
- Obtaining necessary inspections (such as termite and pest as well as overall home inspections).
- Providing the buyer with state and federally required disclosures.
- Opening and shepherding the sale through escrow.
- Clearing title and fulfilling other escrow demands.
- Checking and approving all documents, including escrow forms.

You Get What You Pay For

The purpose for reviewing what's involved in a sale is not to scare you off from doing it yourself. Quite the contrary, in this book we'll go into great detail in demonstrating how you can, indeed, do it yourself. As you will see, it's not impossible, indeed, not even that difficult.

For now, however, it's important to understand that selling a home is a trade-off. If you don't pay a commission, it doesn't mean that you get off scot-free. Rather, it means that you've traded a commission for doing the work yourself. Or you've traded part of a commission for doing part of the work yourself.

Always remember that there's still the work to be done. It's only a question of who's going to do it. Is it worth thousands of dollars to you to do some of it yourself? Increasingly, sellers are answering yes!

It's Not Hard

You do not need a real estate license to successfully sell your own home.

You do not need to be an attorney to successfully sell your own home.

You do not need to be an accountant or other financial guru to successfully sell your own home.

What you do need to be is willing to do at least some of the work, and open to seeking expert guidance in areas where you don't have the expertise. (For most people, that's the paperwork.)

Fortunately, today there's help to be found for almost every need in selling your home, as we'll soon discover in the following chapters.

2

Step-by-Step to Selling Your Own Home

There's no mystery to selling your home on your own. Just do the right things and your house will sell. It's not mind over matter or conjuring arcane spells. It's just following the steps, one at a time.

What are the steps to selling your home? There are ten steps, which we will present here, one at a time and in the proper order.

Step One—Determine What Your Home Is Worth

Do you know what your home is worth?

Most sellers believe they do. After all, most sellers follow the prices in their neighborhood. Whenever a nearby home sells, they check it out—they find out the sales price and then figure how much more their home is worth.

But is this method accurate? Do you really know the value of your home? In truth, very few sellers actually do.

The reality is that most sellers are too emotionally involved with their property. They know how much they paid for it and know the costs of what they put in. They dearly remember the blood, sweat, and perhaps even tears those improvements cost. And, understandably, they want every penny back, plus a profit.

Unfortunately, the truth is that what sellers want for a home has nothing at all to do with what a home is worth—it's worth only what the market will bear. And who knows the market best? Why it's the buyers!

Surprising to most sellers, the fact is that buyers, after only a few days of house hunting, know the market well. After all, they've been looking at every other home that's available. They've been comparing location, size, and features. After a dozen or so homes, they begin to get a pretty good idea of value.

On the other hand, chances are as a seller, you haven't seen all the other homes for sale. You haven't compared locations, sizes, and features. And as a result, you are not up on the market.

You may think your house is worth what the highest-priced house on your street sold for two years ago. You may feel it is worth the sum total of what you've spent on plants, weed control, carpeting, upgrading, and painting. You may feel it is worth what the mortgage appraiser or the county tax assessor evaluated it as.

The most chilling phrase I know of in appraising real estate deals comes when a seller says, "I have a price in mind." The truth is that it doesn't matter what price you have in mind. Your house is worth what the market says it is worth (and what savvy buyers are willing to pay) and not a dime more!

Tough words. But pay heed to them. Nothing keeps a house from selling more than overpricing it.

FSBOs Don't Sell for More

In today's market, price is critical. It is almost as critical as location. Houses that are priced right will sell. Those that are priced too high will sit there. However, the biggest mistake you can make is to think, "Because I'm selling FSBO, I can ask more money for my house."

Of course, you probably won't make this critical error, but if you know of others who are selling FSBO, remind them that buyers see things differently than sellers. Buyers don't care if a house is listed, FSBO, or auctioned. They are interested in only one thing after location, and that's price. Give the buyers the right price and they'll buy.

To you, selling FSBO may be significant. It may mean that you're putting in lots of time and effort. And you may be spending big bucks fixing up the house. It's only natural, therefore, that as a FSBO seller you want to recoup the time, money, and effort from the buyer. It's not unreasonable to feel that you are entitled to ask more for your house.

The truth, unfortunately, is that entitled or not, you can get only what the house is worth on the market. You can ask anything that you want, but you will only get what buyers are willing to pay.

Price it too high, and your house will sit there, languishing, while other homes, priced only a few thousand less, may be sold in days.

How Do I Determine the Right Price?

I hope I've convinced you of the importance to price your home right. But how do you determine what the right price is?

A CMA, or Comparative Market Analysis, allows you to easily determine the correct selling price. With a CMA, you get a list of all of the homes similar to your own that have sold in your area over the past 6 to 12 months. You then compare them by location, size, and features, adding to the value of your house if it is better in some way (a better location) or subtracting if it lacks a feature (such as another home that sold had a swimming pool).

You'll quickly be able to accurately assess what your home is worth in comparison to those that sold. Then you may want to add a few percent if the market is steaming hot, or subtract a few percent if it's stone cold. Thus, you arrive at your correct price.

Where do you get a CMA? Almost any real estate agent will be thrilled to provide one for you. Then call one up, say you are putting your house on the market FSBO, and would like a CMA.

Why would an agent help you when you're selling on your own? Simple: the agent hopes that you'll quickly tire of the effort and then, when you're ready to list, will call on him or her. For an agent, it's simply a service, provided in the hope of getting listings.

Or, you can do your own CMA by using the Internet. Many Internet services (such as <www.smarthomebuy.com>) provide comparables for most homes. At the Web site, you typically can enter your address and, for a nominal fee (usually around $10), you'll quickly get a list of recent sales in your area including location, size, and features. Then you can make your own comparisons.

But be scrupulously honest. Remember, you can't tilt the scales to your favor. Buyers are doing CMAs all the time and they know value. Give them a reasonable price and your house will sell, quickly.

Step Two—Fix Up Your Home

Think of your home as a chocolate cake. You can present this cake in two ways. The first way is to just provide the ingredients. Place flour, water, cocoa, eggs, yeast, sugar, and food coloring in front of most people and they'll look at it dispassionately and say, "Ho Hum." Or you can mix together all the ingredients, bake it, and then present them with the finished product. Their eyes will open wide and they'll say, "Yum, a chocolate cake!"

Homebuyers are no different. Present them with a yard filled with weeds, a front that's got peeling paint, soiled carpeting, scratches on walls, and so on, and they're going to say, "Ho-hum." But if you do the gardening work so that the lawn's mowed and green and the bushes are trimmed with colorful blooming flowers, paint the front, put in new carpeting, get rid of the scratches, and fix it all up, now they'll say, "This is a house I want to buy!"

Make the effort. Do the work. It won't cost too much, take too much time, or be too hard to do. Getting your property ready for buyers is essential if you want to sell. For ideas on what you can do and how much to spend, see Chapter 8.

Step Three—Determine How You Will Handle the Paperwork

Paperwork is the single biggest problem for most people. How are you going to draw up the sales agreement? What about the disclosures and the other documentation needed?

If you're familiar with real estate and have completed many transactions, then this won't seem like such a barrier. But if this is all fairly new to you, then you may be justifiably concerned about getting it right.

Fortunately, as noted in Chapter 1, today there are many options available. Now is the time to decide which you want to use. Look into Chapter 4 on fee-for-service brokers and Chapter 5 on discount brokers. Consider hiring an attorney, if there's availability in your area. See Chapter 13 for the steps to write up your own preliminary sales agreement.

Unless you do it entirely yourself, each of the above arrangements is going to involve spending some money. Budget now. How much are you willing to spend and what do you expect to receive in return?

It's important that you consider these alternatives and make a decision on how you're going to handle the paperwork now. It's too late to start thinking about that when you have a buyer in hand. You might lose that buyer if you appear unsure of yourself at a critical moment.

Step Four—Establish a Contingency Plan

Think of selling your home as a military campaign and you're the general. Any good general is not only going to have a plan A, which he or she hopes will lead to immediate success, but also a plan B on which to fall back upon if plan A doesn't work out.

In the previous step you may have decided, for example, that you're willing to give a 1 percent commission to a discount broker who will handle all of the paperwork for you. However, as we'll see in Chapter 7, for 1 percent the broker may not list the home on the MLS (Multiple Listing Service). Indeed, to get it listed, the discount broker may recommend you pay not only its 1 percent, but an additional 3 percent to a buyer's broker for a total cost of 4 percent to you.

While 4 percent may seem unreasonably high right now, it might not seem so several months down the road *if* your home hasn't sold. So your contingency plan may look like this: List now for 1 percent and give it two full months, during which time you'll advertise and otherwise promote your home (see the next step).

Then, and only then, if the home doesn't sell, call the broker and list it on the MLS.

Why List with the MLS?

Why should listing with the MLS be part of your contingency plan? It doesn't have to be. Your contingency plan could involve listing for 1 percent with a different broker (although because a discount broker typically only provides minimal services, this seems unlikely to help), or taking the home off the market, or renting it out for a time.

However, assuming you want to sell now and are unsuccessful in doing it yourself, you should consider paying more and using the MLS. The reason, quite simply, is that it's important not to try to reinvent the wheel.

Agents use the MLS to work together. There might be as many as a thousand or more agents in your area. If a home is listed on the MLS, it's available to all of them. Because roughly 90 percent of homebuyers first contact an agent, by putting your home on the MLS you are buying into this network.

If for whatever reason you can't sell your house yourself as a FSBO (and we'll look at many reasons and ways to offset these as we go through this book), then it may be time to bite the bullet and buy into the MLS.

Regardless of what your contingency plan is, you should have one. The whole point is to get the house sold, not to have it sit and sit. If plan A doesn't work out in a reasonable amount of time, you're immediately ready to switch to plan B.

Step Five—Prepare a Marketing Campaign

Don't keep the fact that you're selling FSBO a secret. List your house on several of the many online services. If you're not listed with a discount broker (who will give you a sign), get your own sign and display it prominently in your front yard. Prepare leaflets describing your property, including a picture, and distribute them widely. Build an information box and attach it to your sign. (See Chapter 10 for details on how this is done.) Put up flyers on bulletin boards in public buildings, the housing offices of corporations, and even on display panels in supermarkets. And advertise.

Your ad doesn't have to be big, but it should run regularly and you should change it often (so that buyers don't recognize it as the same property and ignore it).

Also, find out whether inexpensive advertising is available on local radio and cable TV stations. (It often is.) Try a 30-second commercial there. The right slant can bring you amazing results. (We'll have much more to say on advertising in Chapter 10.)

Talk up your property to all of your acquaintances whether or not they're interested in buying. Someone may know a friend of a friend who's interested, and that person might ultimately become your buyer.

Finally, be friendly with real estate agents when they come by (and they will!). Tell them that right now you're trying to sell on your own as a FSBO. But if you don't sell within a reasonable amount of time (see the contingency plan above), you'll consider working through them. Tell them that at that point you'll pay a buyer's agent commission if they find a buyer. (See Chapter 7 for details on how a commission is split.)

Talk to agents and be friendly. Remember, they are in the business of finding buyers. It would be foolish to ignore them, particularly when you can get them to work for you.

Step Six—Show Your Home

Making the commitment to sell FSBO means having your home clean and tidy and ready to show at a moment's notice. Unfortunately, it also means giving up much of your free time. It means that you must be willing to sit at home waiting for buyers to show up. If a buyer calls you at eight in the morning on Sunday while you're still sleeping, you'll agree to show the property at nine, even though it means jumping out of bed and working frantically to get the place ready.

Being available for buyers means keeping at least one phone line clear. If you're going to be gone, it means using call forwarding, an answering machine, a cell phone, or a family member to catch incoming calls. It means that you're ready to show the house every day of the week and that it's clean all of those days.

Don't bother to sell FSBO unless you're willing to do all of the tasks described. If you're half-hearted about it, if you decide to take a two-week vacation three weeks after putting the sign in the front yard, if you tell a buyer who calls that you've got to go to your mother's house for lunch and can't show the property, then don't bother to sell FSBO. List.

When you list with yourself, you must make the commitments necessary to sell your home successfully. One of the biggest commitments is time. If you can't spend the time, list with an agent who can. A FSBO seller must show the house. That's just the way it is.

Until you get the appropriate signatures on the dotted line, you're a slave to buyers. To think anything else is to do yourself a disservice. To attempt to sell FSBO without making yourself and the property always available is simply to be playing at it.

If you truly want to sell FSBO, you'll make the time. If you find that you simply can't make the necessary time, then I strongly suggest you reconsider listing with a full-service agent.

Step Seven—Offer Financing

Housing prices today are high and are getting higher. That means that at any given time, the number of people who can qualify for a given house is going down. In short, houses are getting less affordable. (A recent index in California, for example, indicated that in some areas of the state less than 20 percent of buyers could afford the median-priced home!)

This translates into two very powerful problems. First, fewer people have the cash for the down payment necessary for a purchase. Second, even fewer have the income and excellent credit needed to qualify for a big low-down-payment mortgage.

Ideally, you'll probably want the buyer to come in for all cash (meaning a down payment and a new mortgage). However, that may not always be possible. And the easier you can make the purchase for the buyer, the better the chances are that your house will sell before your neighbor's house does.

There is a way you can help the buyer. You can carry back a portion of the sales price (down payment) in the form of a mortgage. Or you can fold most of the buyer's closing costs into a mortgage.

If the buyer doesn't have a lot of cash and can't get a low down payment mortgage, you can help by carrying back 10 percent as a second mortgage. The buyer might put down 10 percent, you'd carry back 10 percent, and then the buyer might be able to qualify for an 80 percent mortgage.

Alternatively, you might carry the buyer's closing costs in a second mortgage. Or, if the lender is willing, agree to a higher sales price with the difference (between the old sales price and the new) folded into the buyer's new, bigger mortgage to cover most of the closing costs. We'll look at these and other financing tricks of the trade in Chapter 14.

The point is that when you make it easier for buyers to purchase, you make it easier on yourself to sell. It's like a pyramid. Those with less money and less income are at the wider bottom. Those with more money and more income are at the pointed top. The more you can appeal to those at the bottom of the pyramid, the bigger the base of potential buyers you can attract.

Step Eight—Hook the Buyer

Some people feel that a good salesperson can sell ice cubes to Eskimos and sunlamps to Hawaiians. If you're this type of salesperson, you can sell your house on your own by next week without my or anybody else's help.

On the other hand, if you're a typical human being, you may get along fairly well with people, but you don't have any supertalents when it comes to selling. Rest assured, you don't need any.

I have found that when selling real estate, or anything else for that matter, the key is to establish a relationship of trust with the person to whom you're selling. Beyond that, the product should sell itself, assuming it doesn't have a problem.

If you establish a working relationship with the buyer and have a good house that the buyer wants, you merely have to nod in the right places, point out the obvious, reassure the faint of heart, and sign on the dotted line. If you have a bad house or the buyer doesn't want it, you're not going to sell it to that prospect now or later, so don't worry about it.

How do you establish trust? Do what comes natural—be honest. (We'll have a lot more to say on how to handle trustworthiness in Chapter 11.)

Step Nine—Know How to Get the Paperwork Done

When you've got your buyer ready to sign on the dotted line, be sure you have a dotted line for him or her to sign on. In Chapter 13, we'll talk about how to work with the buyer to prepare a sales agreement. On the other hand, if you're working with a fee-for-service or discount broker, they should be able to handle the sales agreement for you.

The sales agreement is the most important document of the sale as it governs all the others. Once you have a completed and signed sales agreement, you'll need to open an escrow account (unless an agent is also handling this for you).

There are many escrow companies and you should shop around for the one that offers you the lowest prices. You'll need to pay for escrow services and title insurance for the buyer. Usually an escrow runs for 30 to 45 days. The length of time is determined by need and what's written into the sales agreement. (Who pays what for escrow is determined by local custom—the escrow company can clue you into the usual arrangements in your area.) Chapter 19 provides further details on handling the closing.

Chances are your buyers will want a home inspection and you'll need to provide them with disclosures (and some states require them). See Chapter 15 on disclosures and Chapter 16 on home inspections for more details, and check with any agent who is assisting you for the exact forms required for your state and locale. It is particularly important that you comply with deadlines and disclose all defects. You don't want a buyer coming back years later to hound you over a problem that turned up that you failed to disclose.

Also, should there be any defects in your title, you'll need to clear them up. A defect is something such as a lien you forgot to pay off years ago. Perhaps you were sued by a credit company and they filed against the property. Or perhaps there was a court settlement that was paid off, but the records never reflected it. It's up to you to solve the problem. (Check with an attorney on these issues.)

Step Ten—Close Escrow and Get Your Money

If all goes well (and usually it does), there will come a day when you are notified that escrow is ready to close. For you, as the seller, there's not much more to do than to approve the final escrow instructions (which say who gets paid for what) and sign off on the deed to be given to the buyer.

Finally, when the buyer and the lender deposit funds, the escrow will close and you'll get a call saying your check is ready to be picked up. Chances are it will be one of the best days of your life!

FIGURE 2.1
Your Sales Time Line

3 Days	Step One—Determine What Your Home Is Worth
1-3 Weeks	Step Two—Fix Up Your Home
1 Week	Step Three—Find Someone to Handle the Paperwork
1 Day	Step Four—Have a Contingency Plan
1-2 Months	Step Five—Execute a Marketing Campaign
See Above	Step Six—Show Your Home
See Above	Step Seven—Offer Financing
1-7 Days	Step Eight—Hook the Buyer
30-45 Days	Step Nine—Do the Paperwork
1-2 Days	Step Ten—Close Escrow and Get Your Money

Source: Reprinted by permission of the Mortgage Bankers Association of America.

It Won't Happen All at Once

Rome wasn't built in a day. Most seemingly instant successes are the result of repeated attempts after repeated failures. Most of those who succeed aren't any brighter, more industrious, or more knowledgeable than you.

In short, you too can sell your house FSBO. The trouble is, you may not be able to sell it the first day or the first week, or even the first month. Time may become something you'll learn to hate. You'll stay home on weekends waiting for someone to call or knock on your door. Or, suddenly, three or four people will call and then come by. Or you'll spend so much time cleaning and polishing, painting and trimming that you'll be sick of it. You'll begin to tell yourself you need a vacation from house selling!

In the short term, you may come to hate your house and the process of selling it.

That's okay as long as you don't give up. Hang in there.

3

Can You Really Do It Yourself?

Can you sell your home by yourself?

Everyday people from all walks of life and backgrounds, some with little knowledge of real estate, do it in every state of the union. The real question, of course, is not can you do it, but can you do it easily, quickly, and correctly?

There are lots of fears and concerns, some justified, some not, among homeowners who are considering selling FSBO. Here are just a few of the concerns that I've heard. Are some of these yours?

- I can't understand the paperwork.
- I'm no good at selling.
- How do I handle disclosures?
- I don't have the time.
- It's just too hard.
- It's dangerous to invite strangers into your house.

Maybe you've heard other arguments for not selling your home on your own, but I think these pretty much detail their scope. Basically they are: "I don't know how" and "I'm afraid."

You *Can* Do It

If you want to sell your home as an owner by yourself, you can do it. For every argument against, there are solid reasons why it will work. Let's consider the six concerns previously noted:

1. *Paperwork.* You can always find someone else to do the paperwork for you. This is not to say they'll do it for free; however, for a reasonable fee they'll handle it. On the East Coast, there are some attorneys who handle the paperwork for a fixed and nominal fee. Across the country, there are discount brokers and fee-for-service agents who do nothing else. (See Chapters 4 and 5.)

2. *Salesmanship.* While there are some who seem to be "born" salespeople, I suspect that most of us feel awkward or embarrassed by having to sell something. We feel we could never pressure someone into buying our house. The truth, however, is that good salespeople don't use pressure. They simply present the product (in this case a house) in the best light and let the buyers sell themselves. Now who is more qualified to extol the virtues of your own property than you? (See Chapter 12.)

3. *Disclosure statements.* Today, in almost every home sale, the seller must disclose to the buyer any defects in the property. You must put together a disclosure statement whether you're working with an agent or not, so there's no extra time spent here. (See Chapter 15.)

4. *Time.* Most people think that selling by owner means spending more time. Actually, if you do it right, you can save time in most markets. That's right, a FSBO can move quicker than a listed property.

5. *Too hard.* It's all a matter of perspective. How hard is it not to sell at all? How hard is it to pay a huge commission to an agent? Going through the hoops required to sell by yourself can seem downright easy when compared to those two big "hardnesses."

6. *Strangers.* No one likes strangers in their house. But let's face it, no matter which way you sell, you're going to have

to let strangers see the place. If you do it yourself, you can minimize the risk by showing the property only at reasonable hours and only after qualifying the prospective buyers on the phone, and also by having someone with you for the appointment. More safety tips are included in Chapter 12.

Should You Sell Your Home by Yourself?

As you see, there are reasonable answers to the objections of selling a home "by owner." Plus, there are a number of solid advantages to doing so. Here are four that I think are excellent.

Advantages of Selling by Owner

1. You'll save money. Quite frankly, the reason most people want to sell FSBO is to save the amount they would have to pay on a commission to an agent. As we saw in the first chapter, these commissions are high. You can save all or at least a part by selling yourself.

Note: I'm not saying that agents charge too much. Most in the field work hard and earn every penny. I am simply saying that it's a lot of money to spend if you're a seller, particularly if you can avoid it by doing the work yourself.

2. You'll preserve your equity. Remember, commission is paid out of the equity, even though it's calculated on the sales price. Whether you have a lot of equity or a little, why spend it on commission? Save your equity—sell FSBO.

3. You can get a quicker sale. While most people want to save money by selling by owner, many others simply want a quicker sale. They want to get out of the property as rapidly as possible. One way to do this is to give an amount equal to all (or a portion) of the commission to the buyer. If all the homes like yours are selling for $200,000, instead of listing at that price and paying, for example, a $12,000 commission, simply sell by owner and reduce the price by $12,000 (or less). Suddenly, your home can be 4, 5, even 6 percent below market. Instead of paying a commission to an agent, you're paying an equal amount to the buyer.

It comes out the same to you. However, price-sensitive buyers will swarm to your door for this bargain and your house will sell faster.

4. You can get started investing in real estate. Many well-off real estate investors of today got their start by selling their homes on their own years ago. It taught them how real estate deals are handled. And nothing builds confidence and knowledge more than successfully selling by yourself. Real estate investing careers have to start someplace, and selling FSBO is a great way in.

Why Doesn't Everyone Sell FSBO?

Before you get the impression that selling a home is as easy as falling off a log, rest assured, it's not. If it were, there wouldn't be any agents. Everyone would simply sell their own homes.

Given all the positive reasons to sell by owner, the vast majority of people still fail to do so. A reasonable person has to ask, Why do so many people bypass this alternative and directly list their homes?

First, there's simply the matter of nerve. While few of us would hesitate to have a garage sale to sell almost anything from used clothing to an old piano, or put an ad in the paper to sell the family car, most of us are nonetheless intimidated by the apparently daunting task of selling our own homes. Most people would be happy to conduct the sale of just about any item you can think of by themselves, except their houses. Let's face it, you have to be just a little bit gutsy to sell by owner.

But don't let a lack of nerve stop you from selling FSBO. Remember, it is possible to acquire all the techniques and abilities you fear you don't possess. You can get a buyer to sign a sales agreement. You can get help with the paperwork, the legalities, the negotiations, and even the local customs determining who pays what fees in the transaction.

In short, don't say, "I would like to sell my house by myself. But I don't have the guts to really pull it off!" You can do it.

Another reason for not selling FSBO is the time and effort involved. Many people lead busy, hectic lives and simply don't have the time or energy to devote to selling their homes by themselves. If you're in this group, you're probably not hard to identify. You're the sort who would rather hire a gardener than mow the lawn, take your car to a mechanic rather than change the oil yourself, or call a plumber when you have a leaky faucet rather than buy a washer and fix it.

In short, there are a great many who find it perfectly reasonable to pay a full commission to an agent to do it for them, rather than do the work involved for themselves. If you're in this group, I suggest that you at least read the following chapters to get a sense of what's involved and what you'd be missing.

On the other hand, if you do have the time and energy, by all means spend it getting a quicker sale and/or making more money by selling FSBO. Everything you need to know to do it successfully you can learn from this book.

Remember, there's no law, no custom, no person standing in your way saying that you can't sell your own home. I've owned dozens of properties. Some I've sold through agents. Others I've sold myself. The truth that I've found beyond any author of any book trying to get you to go FSBO, or any agent pressuring you for a listing, is that most people have the ability to sell their homes by themselves, if they really want to.

The Reversible Decision

Trying to decide whether to sell your home (for most people, the largest investment of a lifetime) by yourself or through an agent can be really hard. Therefore, I have an easy way out—a trial FSBO.

If you're not sure whether you'd like to sell FSBO, give it a trial period. Before you list, give yourself a week, a month, two months (probably the most reasonable time period), or whatever. Set a deadline, and until that deadline expires do everything you possibly can to sell by owner. Then, if you still haven't sold the house, you can always list it and have an agent sell it for you.

☑ FIGURE 3.1
Quick FSBO Seller's Self-Test

YES NO (Do you have it in you?!)

❏ ❏ 1. Are you willing to give up evenings and weekends for the next several months?

❏ ❏ 2. Are you willing to let strangers into your home?

❏ ❏ 3. Can you be ready to show your home day or night on a moment's notice?

❏ ❏ 4. Are you willing to learn new and different things?

❏ ❏ 5. Are you determined to save money on your home sale?

❏ ❏ 6. Do you want a quick sale?

❏ ❏ 7. Are you willing to negotiate face-to-face with a buyer?

ANSWERS

1. You have to be ready to show the house when the buyers want to see it. Remember, there's no agent to show it for you.

2. You also have to screen the buyers yourself and then let perfect strangers into your house. If you're overly concerned about security, you're not a good candidate to be a FSBO seller.

3. Spontaneity is needed. A potential buyer who calls wants to see your place *now*. Tell the caller to come back later and you could lose a deal.

4. It's riskier to venture into the unknown and sell FSBO rather than list. But it's also frequently quicker and more profitable.

5. Proper motivation is essential here. If you don't want to save money and sell quickly, why bother selling FSBO?

6. Give the buyer some of the loot and get out quicker.

7. There's no intermediary to blunt the buyer's criticism, anger, or frustration. You have to deal with it all and turn it into something positive.

SCORE
7 = Yes. You're a natural FSBO.
6 = Yes. You need to dwell a little longer on how much money a 6 percent commission really is.
4 to 5 = Yes. Borderline—try it for a while to see if you like it.
1 to 3 = No. Don't waste time. List your house now.

4

Getting Help: Fee-for-Service Agents

If you take your car in for repairs, there is a schedule of fees, usually prominently displayed, of what it costs to fix various parts. There's one charge for rebuilding a transmission, another for grinding engine valves, and so on.

This is called "fee-for-service." It simply means that you pay for what you use. If the service is repairing the thermostat on the car, you only pay the small charge that's involved. You don't pay a big fee for an engine overhaul because that's not what you needed and that's not what you got. The question for us here is, Why can't real estate fees be structured the same way?

Traditionally, the charge for having an agent sell your home has been a commission, a percentage of the selling price. The amount has varied over the years, indeed, there is no set percentage. It's up to the agent and you to negotiate what you're willing to pay.

However, there are usual and customary commission rates charged in most areas. In years past, it was 5 percent. More recently, the rate has been 6 or sometimes even 7 percent.

However, you may not need or want the full services of an agent. You may only want an agent to perform a specific service for you. For example, you may only want the agent to write up

---

FACT

Over the years, agents have upped their rates. They say they need more money to offset higher selling costs. In fact, in 00some areas selling offices add on a "transaction fee" of several hundred dollars in addition to the commission to help pay for their paperwork. From the perspective of the real estate agency—maintaining an office, secretaries, legal consultation, insurance, automobiles, and so on—the commission rates and additional fees seem justified. However, from the perspective of the consumer, they usually seem onerous and high. Because much of the work that an agent does (talking up the property, showing clients around, developing leads, and the like) is not really visible, sellers often don't see all the work that an agent puts in to facilitate a sale. And agents have not always done a good job of making a strong case for their additional costs.

---

the sales agreement. Or perhaps to help you with disclosures. Or to make arrangements for a title search and to open escrow. Or any of a dozen other things involved in a real estate transaction. Why should you pay a full commission, if you only want a limited service?

In the past, you rarely had a choice. Most agents only operated on a commission basis. If you wanted their services, you signed a listing agreement and paid the commission. For that you got all of their services, whether you wanted all of them or not. Your only alternative was to go FSBO, and largely to go it alone.

Enter Fee-for-Service

Today, it's a changing world. Real estate is moving into the new century with a new outlook and many, though certainly not all, agents are responding.

Today, there are agents who recognize that you, as a seller, may not want or need full-service and you certainly don't want to pay for it. They have responded by offering a schedule of fees for individual services that they perform. Now, just as when you take your car into the garage, you need only pay for the service you select.

Where Do I Find a Fee-for-Service Agent?

How difficult it is to find a fee-for-service agent depends on where you live. In Colorado, for example, there are many such agents. In California, they are harder to find. On the East Coast, you can usually find attorneys (discussed shortly) to handle the individual services you need. Typically, the more competitive that the housing market in an area is (the more agents and the quicker the turnover of houses), the more such agents there will be.

An agent often will advertise that he or she offers fee-for-service. Thus, your first course would be to check local newspapers and the yellow pages of the phone book. You might also want to check the Internet because today nearly all agents have some sort of Web presence. However, when you search be sure you include your locale. You may be thrilled that your first search turns up a dozen fee-for-service agents, only to discover they are all located out of state. (Use key words such as "real estate" or "fee-for-service" and your state or city.)

How Do I Evaluate a Fee-for-Service Agent?

You certainly want to be sure that whoever you choose, the person is honest and competent. It would be a horrible mistake to save money hiring a fee-for-service agent only to discover that he or she made a mistake in the documents, or even worse, acted against your best interests.

Qualifying the agent is the same whether he or she is fee-for-service or full service. Following are some things to watch out for.

Does the agent have an office? This may seem simpleminded, but there are agents who work out of their homes or garages. There's nothing wrong with this, except that it usually indicates a certain lack of performance, a lack of success that you should find worrisome. If the agent can't even afford an office, just how good is he or she?

Is the "agent" licensed? In all 50 states, to act as an agent requires passing an exam and obtaining a state license. That doesn't mean, however, that everyone who offers to help you sell your home is, indeed, licensed. Particularly in poorer areas of larger cities, unlicensed people sometimes try to collect fees for real estate services. Any legitimate agent will immediately show you his or her license.

Does the agent belong to a trade organization? The biggest is the NAR (National Association of REALTORS®). It's a step in the right direction if your agent can use the designation, REALTOR.®

Has the agent been in business a long time? Longevity often indicates good business practices. Quite frankly, it's hard for an unscrupulous, dishonest, or incompetent person to stay in business long. Usually, their actions quickly catch up with them (if not the Better Business Bureau and/or the district attorney!). You want an agent who's been in business at least five years. Ask them.

Can the agent provide you with references? Any agent who has been around a while has dealt with hundreds of clients. It should be no problem to provide you with a list (including phone numbers) of a half dozen recent ones. Call a few. Listen to what they say. Did the agent perform as advertised? Was the work of good quality? Was the client satisfied? Most important, would they use the agent again? This is probably your best indicator.

Does the agent have errors and omissions (E&O) insurance? You want to be covered in the event the agent makes a mistake. And the easiest way to be covered is with insurance. Agents normally pay thousands of dollars per year for E&O insurance. If they goof and you sue (or threaten to sue), the insurance company moves in and cleans up the mess. (That doesn't mean you'll automatically be paid for a problem—just that if you have a good case, you stand a better chance of collecting.) Ask to see the agent's policy. Be sure it's current and that it's for a million dollars or more. Keep in mind that agents are not usually required to carry such insurance. If an agent doesn't have it and gets you in trouble, he or she may not personally have the wherewithal to financially handle the consequences. You want an insured agent.

What Should I Expect to Pay?

Fees vary enormously by agent. However, you can expect to pay significantly less than you would for a full-service agent. If you were to use *all* of the services offered, chances are it wouldn't cost you more than around 1 to 2 percent of the sales price. Remember, the agent isn't procuring a buyer.

Here are charges that recently I saw from a fee-for-service agent. Remember, these may be higher or lower than agents charge in your own area.

Clear title problem	$100–500
Closing	250–500
Disclosures	250
Evaluate home inspection	100
Fill out sales agreement	750–1,000
Place advertising	100–???
Open escrow	100
Provide sign	50
Handle phone referrals	250

Obviously, you can pick and choose the ones you want. What's important is that you feel the fees are fair. They should be relative to the service performed. For example, you might expect to pay a larger fee for a sales agreement and a much smaller one for providing a sign. Overall, however, you don't want to pay more in individual fees than you would end up paying if you simply hired a full-service agent. (Or used a discount broker—see Chapter 5.)

Why Would an Agent Offer Fee-for-Service?

That's a good question to ask yourself. If your house is worth $300,000, a full-service commission is about $18,000. Why would a legitimate agent exchange the chance at that big commission for a few thousand dollars in fees?

There are many reasons. Perhaps one of the most common is that the agent hopes to get into your confidence so that, in the event you can't sell your property FSBO, you'll then list full-service with him or her. In other words, the fee-for-service is a sort of "loss leader." Yes, the agent will perform the services, if needed. But the agent's big hope is that you'll sign up for the services when you first start as a FSBO and later, when things don't pan out, you'll come back and list.

There's nothing at all wrong with this. In fact, it's nothing more than a smart marketing ploy on the part of the agent.

On the other hand, maybe the agent is offering fee-for-service because he or she can't get any listings or make any sales. Perhaps it's a desperation move to stay in business. If that's the case, do you really want the services of this person? (Reread the paragraphs above on evaluating your agent.)

Finally, perhaps the agent truly likes a fee-for-service business. It's clean and the money is immediate. The agent doesn't have to spend hours and days driving clients around or cozying up to sellers only to get nothing for the time and effort when they don't buy or sell through him or her. Here the agent performs the service and gets paid. It's neat, quick, and clean, and a good agent can make a nice living at it, even at the reduced fees.

When Do You Pay?

Typically, you pay when the service is performed. However, if you're going to use a fee-for-service agent, it's a good idea to line up the person well in advance of need. When you have a buyer in hand and need a quick sales agreement is not the time to start looking for an agent. (You certainly won't have time to do a proper evaluation.)

Find the agent early on and establish a relationship. Most agents won't want anything from you. And they'll give you a verbal commitment that when it comes time, they'll be ready to serve you.

Some agents will want you to sign an agreement to work with them and to put up a small retainer, sometimes as little as $100. This locks you in to them. However, I don't really see any advantage to you to do this. Further, if it turns out that you never need the agent's services, you're out the hundred bucks!

What about Using an Attorney?

Many people do and, as noted earlier, on the East Coast there are many fine real estate attorneys who have long performed in a fee-for-service manner, typically under $1,500 for an entire transaction. However, in most of the country, you will be hard-pressed to find an attorney who specializes in real estate. Instead, most are general-purpose lawyers who will handle this for you for at their regular hourly rates. These rates easily can be as much as several hundred dollars an hour. Because these attorneys don't do this sort of work on a regular basis, you may find they take longer (must look things up) and may not do as good a job as someone who does it day in and day out.

Further, if you'll glance back at some of the services performed on the list above, you'll note that not all are really suited to attorneys. While filling out a sales agreement or creating or reviewing documents may be ideal for an attorney to do, answering buyers' phone calls or providing a For Sale sign are not. In fact, most of the services you're likely to want are best performed by an agent, not an attorney.

Finally, because good agents are involved in real estate transactions on a daily basis, they often know the best way of handling things. There have been many cases in my own experience where, even though it was a legal matter, I'd prefer the common-sense services of an agent over the legalese an attorney might provide.

Are Agents Legally Authorized to Offer Fee-for-Service?

This moves into a gray area that is difficult to answer. In most states, a licensed agent is *not* supposed to provide legal services. For that you need an attorney. But what is a legal service?

Most certainly it's not providing you with a sign, answering phone calls from prospective buyers, or holding an open house. But what about filling out documents, for example, a sales agreement, the most important document in a transaction?

In most states today, an agent may not construct a sales agreement from scratch. An attorney must do that. However, most states allow an agent to fill in the blanks on a previously attorney-prepared sales agreement. In other words, the agent can enter the names of the parties, the address of the property, and the terms of the financing. For the rest, there's usually a series of paragraphs that either the seller or the buyer must check. And typically you are advised to seek legal counsel before doing so.

F A C T

Sales agreements today are often many pages long. It is not unusual to find one that extends for as many as ten pages. The "boilerplate" covers the many different situations you and the buyer might find yourself in and provides a way of dealing with them. They lock you and the buyer together. These documents are intended to be legally binding on both buyer and seller and should not be entered into lightly. You want a good document that protects your interests. Remember, if the sale goes well, you really don't need all that protection. If the sale goes badly, however, you'll need all the protection you can get.

If that's the case, what do you need the agent for? Can't you fill in the blanks yourself?

There is the matter of simply getting the form. In California, for example, the sales agreement provided by the California Association of REALTORS® specifies that it must not be filled out by anyone other than an agent. And usually it will only be provided to agents.

Most national real estate companies (CENTURY 21,® Coldwell Banker, Prudential, and the like) have their own forms, and they usually will not provide them to you to use. They are strictly for their own agents.

Finally, the forms you typically can find at stationery stores often provide only minimal boilerplate and need to be expanded to be effectively used in your area. You may be taking a real chance by using them.

Thus, when you get a fee-for-service agent filling out a sales agreement, you're not only getting the agent, but the agreement as well!

Should You Use a Fee-for-Service Agent?

It's up to you whether you want to use a fee-for-service agent. But keep in mind that only a few years ago there were virtually no such agents around. You didn't have the option.

Today, in many areas you do. And in the future, we may find the fee-for-service agent becoming more the rule than the exception.

5

Getting Help: Discount Brokers

All real estate brokers do not work the same way. Some are the traditional broker who simply will not work for less than "full" commission, typically 6 or 7 percent.

However, recently a new type of broker has emerged who will work for less—a discount broker. Discount brokers are now seen across the country working both independently and as franchisees for national chains.

While negotiating a lower fee has always been at least theoretically possible with any real estate broker, even the most traditional, these discount brokers make it easy. You don't have to negotiate for it. They offer a discounted fee right up front. Even more astonishing, a few will even provide full service for the discounted fee!

To see how their discount works, we first need to understand the fee structure in general use for agents in real estate.

How Agents Get Their Commission

When you hire an agent for a 6 percent commission, that particular agent almost never receives the entire 6 percent. Rather, the commission is usually split between several real estate brokers and, possibly, several salespeople. Here's what a typical split would look like:

Traditional Commission Split

Total Commission	6%	$12,000 on a $200,000 sale
To selling broker	1.5%	$ 3,000
To selling salesperson	1.5	3,000
To buyer's broker	1.5	3,000
To buyer's salesperson	1.5	3,000

Thus, the real estate company (broker) that represents the buyer splits the commission in half with the real estate company (broker) that represents the seller.

Then each real estate company (broker) splits what they get with the salespeople who represent the buyer and seller.

Thus, the agent who represents you as a seller, if he or she is only a salesperson and not a full broker, may only get 1.5 percent of a 6 percent commission ($3,000 on a $12,000 commission).

Of course, there are exceptions to the rule. If the salesperson is very good (sells lots of properties), he or she can negotiate with the broker for a higher percentage. Top salespeople often get 80 to 90 percent of the half commission (3 percent) that their brokers get.

How Does a Discount Broker's Commission Work?

As noted, the broker representing the seller typically gets half the commission (3 percent out of 6 percent). A discount broker will accept less than that 3 percent.

How much less?

The amount could be either a flat fee or a percentage. Some discount brokers work for as little as $1,000 a home. Others want $3,000 to $4,000 as a flat fee.

On the other hand, some discount brokers want a percentage. These may vary from a low of about 1 percent to a high of around 2.5 percent.

FACT

A broker is a licensed real estate agent able to operate an independent (or franchised) office. A salesperson is a licensed real estate agent who must serve an apprenticeship under a broker, usually for two years. A salesperson may not operate an office on his or her own. Sometimes brokers will choose to work for another broker. If they are very good, they can command a higher percentage of the broker's take on the commission, as much as 90 percent of 3 percent. The term "agent" refers to any broker or salesperson.

Thus, instead of paying the broker who represents you the traditional 3 percent, you pay them significantly less. The savings to you can be substantial.

**Discount Savings on a $200,000 Commission
Otherwise at 6 Percent**

Percent Discount Broker Gets	You Save
1 %	$4,000
1.5	3,000
2	2,000
2.5	1,000

How Can a Broker Afford to Offer Such a Discount?

In some cases, it's because the discount broker doesn't perform all of the services of a full-service broker. (This is not always the case, as we'll see shortly.)

For example, the discount broker may not do one or more of the following:

- Show the property
- Advertise
- Promote the property to other agents
- Field calls from prospects

The discount broker almost always will, however, provide a sign and do the paperwork involved in the transaction for you (including writing up the sales agreement). In other words, you are largely on your own when it comes to finding a buyer. But once found, the discount broker will help you complete the transaction.

Are There Discount Brokers Who Are Full-Service?

There's an old wag about a person who's selling hot dogs on a street corner for 50 cents apiece. A woman comes up to him and asks, "How can you sell the hot dogs so cheaply? You have to buy the meat, the bun, the condiments. Surely it must cost you much more than two quarters just to buy the ingredients." The man answered, "I make it up on volume!"

An old joke, but what if the hot dog salesman had a way to obtain the ingredients much more cheaply. Could he make it up on volume? Perhaps so!

This is the position of "Assist2Sell," a relatively new discount brokerage company out of Reno, Nevada. Assist2Sell claims nearly 150 franchise offices across the country. And it says it is able to sell real estate and provide full service for less than traditional agents.

The company generally (each franchisee operates somewhat differently) offers advertising, answers phone calls, and shows property in addition to handling documents and managing escrow. It does all of this for a fee structure ranging from $1,500 to $4,000 per home.

It provides this service by paying salespeople a flat fee that is typically much lower than the commission they might otherwise receive. Additionally, the broker's office also makes a much lower fee. However, by putting through many more deals, they claim to make it up on volume.

Assist2Sell says it provides:

- Advertising
- Fields phone calls
- Shows your property

It apparently, however, does this primarily through its own network of agents. It will not list your home on the MLS (Multiple Listing Service) for the discount fee structure. However, because its agents are REALTORS,® it can list on the MLS, *if* you are willing to pay the buyer's agent commission.

Will the Discount Broker Put My Home on the MLS?

The MLS, you'll recall, is the tool used by brokers to share listings. One broker puts his or her listing on the MLS and then all can work on it.

> # FACT
>
> Assist2Sell is not so much a helper to the FSBO seller, but a full-service agent offering its services for less money.

The MLS is without question the best and quickest way of finding a buyer for your home. Today, more than 90 percent of all homebuyers work with agents. (Remember, it doesn't cost them anything because you're paying the commission!) And those agents work the MLS looking for properties. Thus, if your home is listed there, you immediately have access to 90 percent of the buyers in your area. (There may be thousands of agents working off the MLS in any given area.)

In many cases, discount brokers are also REALTORS® (members of the National Association of REALTORS®) who operate the MLS throughout the country. Thus, if you request it (and you should!), they will put your home on the service so you can partake of the advantages the service offers.

However, the discount broker will not share his or her commission on the MLS. Remember, you're only paying a seller's agent commission here. To take real advantage of the MLS, you must also be willing to pay a commission to the buyer's agent. The question then becomes, How big a commission should that be?

How Much Should I Pay a Buyer's Agent?

Remember, the usual buyer's agent fee is half, or roughly 3 to 3.5 percent, of the full 6 or 7 percent commission. When you have your discount broker list your home on the MLS, you can specify that amount, or anything less. For example, you can offer to pay a buyer's agent only 1 percent. (At 1 percent to the buyer's agent and, for example, 1 percent to the discount broker you're using, that's a total of 2 percent you would owe.)

I discourage you from doing that, however. Here's why: The buyer's agent is supposed to represent the buyer's best interest. That means showing the buyer the house most suited to his or her needs, *regardless* of how big or small a commission is involved. Knowing this, you may be inclined to offer the lowest possible buyer's agent commission.

But there's also human nature at play here. Consider a buyer's agent who has a client who wants to buy a house. Your home would be perfect. But that agent reads down the MLS listing and sees that you're only offering a 1 percent commission.

Right next to your listing is another home similar to yours. But that other home's seller is offering a 3 percent commission. If you were that agent, whose home would you show? Would you show the one on which you could make a 1 percent commission (probably split with a broker) or 3 percent?

It's important to remember that in real estate you're in competition with all the other homesellers. And unless you meet the competition, you'll probably not be successful in selling.

Therefore, I suggest that you either try to sell on your own FSBO (and just use the limited services of a discount broker for the paperwork, a sign, and whatever else they may provide), or bite the bullet and pay the full buyer's agent commission. That's the best way to accomplish your true goal of selling your home.

Set a Time Limit

I believe the best way of handling these sometimes torturous decisions is to let time do it for you. Begin by deciding to sell FSBO. (I believe every seller ought to at least give this a shot.)

You can be a purist and do it entirely on your own. Or if you're like most people and are unsure of handling the paperwork, you can hire a discount broker (at 1 percent or so) to do that for you.

Then set a deadline. You'll try FSBO for a month, or two months, or however long you arbitrarily decide. And give it your best shot. Using the techniques outlined in this book, make every effort to come up with a buyer.

But if after your own self-imposed time limit expires and you still don't have a buyer, put your property on the MLS. Pay the fees. Get it sold.

FACT

Many FSBO sellers waste a lot of time by being stubborn if they are initially unsuccessful in selling their home. Instead of listing, and getting their home sold and moving on, they persist in trying to sell FSBO. They may waste months, sometimes even years, when they could have sold through an agent and moved on with their lives. Remember, your true goal is to sell your home, not to save on a commission.

How Do I Find a Good Discount Broker?

The rules are pretty much the same as for finding a good full-service agent. You can check with friends and relatives for a reference. Often hearing that someone had a wonderful experience with a particular agent is the best recommendation you can get.

If you don't know anyone who has a good contact, then try the tried and true methods. Check the yellow pages of the phone book. Check the advertising in the newspaper.

For discount brokers, however, often the best source is the Internet. I've found that most maintain a strong Web presence with a Web site that will describe the discount service they offer. Probably the most popular discount brokers operating on a national basis as of this writing include: <www.assist2sell.com> and <www.helpusell.com>.

What Should I Watch Out for When Selecting a Discount Broker?

There are a number of pitfalls to avoid when selecting a discount broker to work with you. Following are five common ones.

1. Bait and switch. Be wary of the discount broker that lures you in with promises of a lower cost, then tries to convert you to a full commission. Once you begin talking with the agent, you may discover that there are few services for the discounted fee and the agent emphasizes that you're unlikely to really sell your home using the discount plan. However, if you move up to full-service, at full commissions, you're much more likely to get a sale, and quickly. If this happens, feel free to walk out. Remember, if you want to pay a full commission, you don't need a discount broker.

2. Up-front fees. It doesn't matter if you're paying a reduced commission or a flat fee—the agent should not get paid until your home sells. No sale, no fee/commission to the agent. Beware of discount brokers who want their fee up front. Once paid, they may not deliver even minimal services. (The exception here is advertising where you may agree to pay a portion for a reduced fee. However, be sure you control the ads and all your money goes toward them.)

3. Lack of REALTOR® status. As discussed earlier, to put your home on the MLS, the agent must usually be a REALTOR.® Thus, you'll

want to be sure he or she has this designation. Further, REALTORS®
are members of the National Association of REALTORS,® an organization that helps promote professionalism in the field.

4. Independent broker or franchisee. There may be some added
protections when dealing with a franchise. It may use standard-
ized forms (including a purchase agreement) and there may be
policies that are put in place to protect you. A lot depends, of
course, on how strictly the local franchisees are overseen by
the franchise company. On the other hand, there may be some
advantages to dealing with an independent. For example, the
broker may more easily be able to design a package to conform
to your needs. And the independent broker can negotiate freely
on services performed and commission fees without a franchise
company dictating specific policy.

5. A large market presence. Does the discount broker you're
thinking of dealing with regularly run advertisements in the local
newspapers (either by office or by franchise)? Does it run ads on
the radio and television? What about a significant Web presence?
The more of the market the broker can attract, the greater the
chances that your discount broker can actually come up with a
buyer for your property. Remember, if you've already agreed to
pay a buyer's agent commission, there's no reason the listing discount broker can't pick that up, if he or she finds a buyer for you,
in addition to his or her seller's agent fee.

FACT

In real estate, there are very few wholly owned offices.
Most companies, including most of the largest, franchise out
their name to individual brokers to use.

6. Longevity and references. Of course, as with the fee-for-service agent discussed in Chapter 4, or with any full-service broker, it goes without saying that you should ask how long they've been in business and if they can provide references. Remember, five years' full-time experience is what I consider a minimum. Any less and the agent is learning on you.

F A C T

Many agents only work part-time. They may be receiving money from a retirement fund, or they may have another part-time job. Part-time agents, though usually well-intentioned, may not have the experience you need to successfully conclude a sale.

And remember to ask for references. An active agent should be able to provide you with half a dozen references from property sales they've participated in over the past six months. (If the agent can't provide you with many recent references, you have to seriously ask yourself why not?)

Call the references. Too often sellers will get a list and be satisfied just to have it. They'll assume that by being able to provide the list, the agent has satisfied the reference requirement.

Not so. Until you call, as far as you know the list could have been taken right out of the phone book.

You don't need to call all of the references, but pick at least three at random. You'll want to ask them the usual questions:

- Did the agent successfully sell your home?
- Were there any problems? Did the sale go quickly?
- Would you list with the agent again?

Let your decision on whether to choose this discount broker come from the answers you receive.

6

Getting Help: Online Listing Services

The newest way to sell your home by yourself is online using the Internet. However, if you don't have a computer or you don't want to handle an electronic sale, don't feel bad—you're still in the vast majority.

Most people continue to sell the old-fashioned way with a sign in the front yard and ads in the local newspaper. If that's your preference, then just continue on. You can complete a successful FSBO sale without ever turning on a computer.

On the other hand, if you want to get ahead of the curve and you're even a little computer literate, read on. In this chapter, we'll learn how to successfully use the Internet to list your house and pull in buyers.

Do People Really Buy Homes on the Internet?

Hard statistics are difficult to come by, but given the rapidly increasing numbers of online listings available, it would seem that this is the newest and fastest growing source of buyers.

For example, the Internet listing service, Realtor.com, claims to have more than a million listings drawn from real estate boards across the country. Listings often offer a picture of the property and a thorough description, as well as a broker contact. Of course, this service is only open to agents, but if selling online is good enough for the agents, it should be good enough for FSBO sellers.

But, you may be wondering, who shops for a home on the Internet? Don't most people go out with agents, drive neighborhoods looking for homes, or simply peruse the local newspaper?

Certainly, all of the above are the traditional means of finding the perfect home. But increasingly, people are also (sometimes as a first choice) checking out the Internet. First among these are buyers relocating to a new area. If you're moving from New York to Los Angeles, it's a lot easier and cheaper to first explore the new area via the Internet than it is to fly there, rent a hotel room and car, and go looking around. I recently was working with a buyer who was in Paris, France, and wanted to purchase a home in Philadelphia. What better way to look than over the Internet?

On the Web, the potential relocator can discover dozens of different cities and neighborhoods in a few minutes. By seeing pictures of the home as well as comparing prices, the buyer can very quickly narrow the field. Thus, when that buyer does fly across the country to look, he or she may have already made contact with you and may be ready to physically examine your house.

Of course, Internet homebuyers aren't limited to relocators. These days all sorts of people use the Internet for just about everything from buying autos to books. As I was writing this, for example, through an ad on the Internet a neighbor sold his bicycle to a buyer in a city 150 miles away.

Potential homebuyers who live in your state, city, or even your neighborhood, may first turn to the Internet to see what's available around them. If your house is listed prominently, they may decide to e-mail or call you. And you could be on your way to a sale.

An estimated 100 million people use the Internet on a regular basis. With that kind of patronage, it's a potential source for buyers that you simply can't ignore.

How Do I Get Started?

There are three elements to selling a home online:

1. Listing your house electronically
2. Converting inquiries to real buyers
3. Concluding the sale

We'll cover all three here, primarily concentrating on the first two. Before we begin, let's be sure that we understand what's required to sell your house online. First, you must have a computer. And you must be able to access the Internet.

What Do I Need?

Your computer doesn't have to be the fastest or the most powerful, but it must have a modem and it should have the fastest modem connection currently available. Otherwise, you may find that it simply takes too long and is too tedious to send images for your FSBO listing. Because computers are upgraded so rapidly and so radically, rather than give specific computer minimums, let's just say that you need a fully equipped computer that's no more than about a year old. If you have that, you should be all set.

You also must have access to the Internet. At a minimum, all you need is an ISP (Internet service provider) such as AOL (America Online), MSN (Microsoft Network), or one of many others. If you want to create your own Web page, most of these services let you do it. Or you can buy a domain—a sort of home to call your own on the Internet—and do it yourself. There are services that will help you do this for a fee.

To create a really fancy Web site, you'll need a publishing program such as Microsoft's Front Page, Adobe's PageMill, Macromedia's Dreamweaver, or one of the many others. However, if you just want a bare-bones page, you can create a perfectly acceptable listing using tools already available on the Web. You'll also want to use one of the many services that will ensure your Web page is posted with the many search engines available. This makes it easier for buyers to find you.

Finally, we're going to assume that you already know how to dial up your ISP and get onto the Internet. If not, there are many books and articles available that will get you started.

Doing It

As in all things in life, it's most important to keep focused on your goal. In terms of listing your house on the Internet, the goal is getting potential buyers to see your listing. You can have the most elaborate listing in the world with fancy downloadable video walkthroughs, but if nobody ever finds your site, who's to know? Being great, but obscure, may be okay for poets and artists, but it's definitely not the way to go if you want to sell your home.

The easiest way to get your house on the Internet is to list it with an existing service. There are dozens of these, and the advantage they offer is that you don't have to do any work—there's no Web page to create. Just type "FSBO" into any search engine (such as Yahoo!, Excite, or Lycos) and you'll instantly get a huge list of such services.

Remember, just as you can find these services easily, so can potential buyers. Listing services make it a point to be easily noticed. It's a great way to get your house on the Web with an absolute minimum of effort.

Can I List for Free?

Yes and no. Some services offer you a minimum listing free as a come-on. But if you want to expand it or put in a picture, there most likely is a charge.

The best way to judge whether you'd like to be listed on a service is to pretend you're a buyer. Go to the service and locate the city you're in. Click to see "by owner" listings in your area. If there are many, chances are you've got an active service.

Also check to see that the listing gives you at least the basics: price, number of bedrooms and baths, and a few other items.

Next, check to see if a picture is available. Remember, a picture is worth a thousand words. Nothing helps sell a listing like an image of the house. Without a picture, the buyer only has dry words to convince him or her to check further. You want a service that will put up a picture.

Should I Pay a Fee to List My House on the Internet?

It could be worthwhile, and it has the advantage of being an easy way to go. Providing the service you choose is easily found and does a good job, it might produce some real buyers for you. After all, you're going to have to spend some money no matter what. There's the cost of a sign for the front yard and advertising in the newspapers. Consider this a similar expense.

If you decide to list with a service, the cost can range from as little as $25 to more than $175. When considering taking the plunge, there are some questions you'll want to ask the FSBO listing service, which we'll detail next.

How easy is the service to find? You're the best judge of this. Did you find it easily? If so, chances are so will someone else, hopefully a buyer.

Does it serve my area? All real estate is local. You want a service that specializes in your particular neck of the woods. Some services claim to cover the entire country. However, in my experience, when I try them and look up a particular city, I almost always find a message that says something like, "No Listings for This City." In other words, they may have an index that covers every city in the country, but their database for your area may be virtually empty. Most homebuyers in your area will quickly discover this and be turned off by the service.

The other side of this argument is that if you're the only listing in a particular city, then every potential buyer who hits on the service looking for your city will find only your listing. You'll get all the attention.

While this may be true, I think buyers are looking for services with lots of listings so they can get the feeling they're dealing with an active market.

Many listing services focus on a particular area: Seattle, for example, or the San Francisco Bay Area, New York, or just about anywhere else. Quite frankly, when I'm buying, I first look for the listing service that specializes in the area where I want to live.

How easy is it to deal with the service? Is it user friendly? If I supply a photo of my house (an absolute minimum), can they include it on my listing? How many photos? How many words can I use? How prominent will my listing be among all the others?

You need to ask these questions and feel comfortable with the answers.

How successful is the service? Ideally, the listing service should be able to provide a list of successful homesellers, along with e-mail addresses or telephone numbers so you can contact them.

Barring that, you should check to see how many listings the service has. Use a search engine to find a listing service in your area. Are there ten homes listed? Twenty? None? A local service should be crammed with listings.

How long will the listing last? Many services charge by the month. Your listing is deleted after 30 days if you don't pay another up-front fee. While you hope to sell within 30 days, it may take longer. Factor that in when you calculate the charge. The service may only be $50 per month, but after four months you're already up to $200.

Should I list with multiple services? It's probably a good idea. That way you increase your exposure. The problem is that you also increase your expense. If you can find free listings, of course, hop on board.

Should I give my credit card number online? Leading retailers (such as airlines and mail-order dealers) use any of several encryption services for accepting credit cards online. My personal experience is that these services have been safe for me. However, many smaller listing services do not offer these safeguards. I suggest that if you're going to pay for a service, telephone the provider and give your credit card number and other financial information over the phone.

What about Creating My Own Web Page Listing?

Creating your own Web page is not hard and it doesn't need to cost you anything beyond the software and some time. Quite frankly, the easiest way to do this is to subscribe to one of the service providers that offers a free home page to its subscribers (and many do) and then use its Web publishing tools to create your page. Thus, it doesn't cost you anything and usually takes very little time.

Let's take AOL as an example because they're the biggest. AOL's Personal Publisher is available as a free service and is extraordinarily easy to use; you don't need to know HTML (hypertext markup language—the computer language of the Internet) to use it, and the results, while not unique, may be more than adequate for your needs.

A few words about AOL: The server has been amply criticized in the past for poor service—the inability of many subscribers to get online when they wanted. While I'm sure much of this criticism was deserved, the service has vastly improved. The fact remains that as of this writing, AOL is the most widely used ISP in the United States with more than 20 million subscribers. Whether or not you like AOL, it provides an excellent, cheap opportunity to list your property.

How Do I Do It on AOL?

It couldn't be simpler. Log on to AOL, click on "Internet" and then "Internet Extras." The first listing is Personal Publisher. (This is the path as of this writing; however, as technology is constantly changing and upgrading, it may be different by the time you use it.)

You will find a variety of options, including many explanations for how to use Personal Publisher. When you're ready, click on "Create a Page" and begin. Be sure to opt for a "business" page as opposed to a "personal" page, as you'll find the business options more suited to your needs.

A wizard (interactive tutorial) will take you through some very easy steps. You'll be asked for such things as a title and filler material. You'll also be offered a chance to add your own picture.

Finally, after you've created a page just the way you want it, you'll be able to "publish" it. In other words, you'll be able to upload it to the Internet where potential buyers can find it.

What If I Want a More Elaborate Web Page?

Creating an elaborate Web page is not that hard. First, you'll need a place on the Internet to call home, a domain, a dedicated URL (Universal Resource Locator). You'll need to register your name and get your own Web address. A number of services will handle this for you. Check with a good search engine for current services.

Registering your name currently costs around $35 for a year. Your name must be different from any other on the Internet (just as your street address must be different from any other). If you have a name you want to use (perhaps your own name), you can do a quick check to see if anyone else is using it by simply typing in the desired address as a location to find on Netscape, Explorer, or whatever Internet browser you are using.

If this check doesn't turn anything up, you're probably home free, although there are sites on the Web that are registered but are inactive. Be sure to check the various options available such as yourname.com, yourname.org, or yourname.net, or the many new extensions coming online.

If a name you want to use is registered as .com but not .net, you may still be able to use it, but it may prove confusing for someone trying to reach you. It's probably better to have a completely distinct name. There are also sites that register your desired name for a minimal fee, and they perform a more thorough search.

Once you get a domain name, you'll need a server to service it, to handle the computer logistics of actually putting a presence on the Internet. Often, the same company that helped you register will offer this service, typically for less than $25 a month.

Once I Have a Site, How Do I Create a Page?

Now you need to construct a home page and, if you desire, additional pages. To accomplish this, you'll need to use a Web editor. This is a program that actually builds the page in your computer and then, when it's the way you want it, publishes (uploads) it to the Net at your site. It also allows you to make changes as needed afterward.

There is a wide variety of such programs to choose from including PageMill from Adobe, FrontPage from Microsoft, or Dreamweaver from Macromedia. They all have the ability to quickly—though not necessarily easily—get your Web page constructed. Most such programs are transparent with HTML, which means you don't need to know Internet language to use them. Some also offer wizards that lead you through by the hand so that it's almost impossible to make a mistake.

What Should I Say in My Listing?

Assuming that you're using a free Web page on a service such as AOL, or are constructing your own Web page for your own URL, the next question is how to attract buyers. What do you say to induce people to contact you and, hopefully, make a purchase?

The Heading

The heading should include the fact that your home is for sale by owner. Simply stating "FSBO" or "By Owner" should be sufficient.

Next, include the best selling feature of the property. Perhaps it's the size, location, view, or price. For example, you might want to say, "FSBO—SEE THE WHOLE CITY."

The Text

For the copy, you'll want to include the basics: price, location, size, best features, and special inducements, and be sure to include both your e-mail address and your phone number.

An important point to remember is that the person reading your listing may not be at all familiar with the area. It would be wise to spend some time writing up the location (perhaps include a map). Indicate the quality of the schools and their proximity. Tell them how close you are to shopping and expressways. Try to give the flavor of the area. Is it rustic with lots of trees; suburban with a community pool; or a big city with all the attached excitement?

Remember, it's the sizzle that sells, not the steak. Try to imagine would-be buyers of your home and create copy as appealing to them as possible.

Chapter 10 includes more tips on how to write copy that will attract buyers.

Be Careful of Typefaces

If you're putting up a listing on a free Web page, such as AOL, this isn't a concern. But when designing your own Web page, there's the temptation to use fancy type to attract attention.

On your Web editor, you type in words just as you would in a word processor. You can make your words large or small, bold or italic. And most Web editors also give you a wide range of fonts.

Keep in mind, however, that the fonts the user sees are determined by his or her computer, not yours. Your Web page communicates the content and the computer used by the person visiting your site fills in the fonts. In other words, if you choose a font that is not resident (already installed) on the user's computer, then that computer will substitute something else in its place. This can drastically alter the look of your site. Thus, it's usually best to use only standard fonts, such as Helvetica or Times Roman, that are common to most computers.

How Do I Get a Picture in My Listing?

As I previously noted, a picture is worth a thousand words. Nothing helps sell your home better than a picture of it. Potential buyers can immediately see if it's the type of home they are looking for. Ideally, you'll use pictures of the front of the home, as well as the interior and the views the home offers.

AOL and similar free Web page providers offer you the opportunity to include pictures. Take advantage of it. If you've got your own domain, put up lots of pictures.

Where Do I Get the Pictures?

You have to take them yourself. If you have a camcorder or digital camera, getting the picture is simple. Shoot the images you want, then download them to your computer. If you're using a digital camera, you already know the procedure—it came with the software sold with your unit. Today's modern camcorders often offer the same downloading capability as digital cameras, making it quite simple.

If you don't have an electronic camera of some sort, then any film or slide camera will do. Take the pictures you want and have the film developed. Either scan them yourself or take the developed pictures to an imaging center that has a scanner. These days there are dozens in most cities (check the yellow pages). The imaging center will scan the photos for you and create digital files.

What Type of Graphics File Should I Use?

You can choose from a variety of file types such as .TIF, .TGA, or others. Each has a different characteristic and is used for different purposes. The software that comes with a digital camera or camcorder typically can create a JPEG (JPG—Joint Photographic Expert Group) image. This is fine because it compresses the information in the image into a much smaller size, making it more easily transferable to the Internet.

The formats you want to use for the Web are primarily GIFs and JPEGs. GIF (Graphics Interchange Format), created by Compuserve, was designed specifically for use on the Internet. The biggest enemy of the Internet is time. It takes time to transmit files. You don't want a user to be kept waiting too long for a picture of your house to be transmitted to their computer, or they may simply go elsewhere.

Because a GIF is a compressed format, it minimizes the file transfer time across the phone lines. Thus, it's ideal for your purposes.

JPEG is also a compressed format; however, it allows you to specify the degree of compression used. The higher the compression, the sharper the image. If you're using an ISP, you have to be sure that the compression you use will be accepted. Also, you must be sure that the program you are using is capable of creating JPEG files (most imaging programs do).

Ideally what you want is to get the smallest file possible for your graphics so that the image will be transmitted to your potential buyer as quickly as possible.

Once you have your photograph ready to go as a graphics file in your computer, you'll need to publish it. If you're using an ISP such as AOL, log onto its Web editor and find the control that lets you send a graphics file from your computer to theirs. Keep in mind that not all services allow you to add a photo. If you've got your own domain, use your own Web editor to publish your graphics files.

What about Embellishing My Page?

You want to attract buyers and you can and should use all of the colors, textures, backgrounds, and other features that the world of advertising has led us to expect from good looking ads. Of course, if you're just listing with a service or using the free Web page of an ISP, you probably won't have many options, if any at all.

But if you've got your own domain and Web editor, the sky's the limit.

And that's really all there is to it.

List your house online. It's fun to do. It can't hurt. And the way the Internet is growing, it could net you a buyer.

7

Getting Help: Commission Cutters

When you're selling FSBO, it's important to decide early on whether you're a purist, or whether you're willing to get help from the powers that be. I'm speaking of working within the existing system of real estate agents.

Of course, it all comes down to money. Agents want money for their services. In the previous chapters, we've seen how to pay less by using either a fee-for-service agent or a discount broker. But that's only on the selling end. What about on the buying agent's end? What about the broker who represents a buyer?

Can I Work Directly with the Buyer's Broker?

Often, you'll find that when you receive an offer on your home, it comes not from the buyer but through an agent. Okay, you may be saying. That's no skin off my nose.

But it is. The buyers will want *you* to pay their agent's commission!

How can that be?, you may be asking yourself. The buyers go out and secure an agent and then they want me to pay for it? Ridiculous.

Perhaps. Nevertheless, that's often the way things work out. The agent will come to you and say he or she has a buyer for your home. They're pretty sure the buyer will go for the property. However, to make the sale you'll have to pay the agent a commission.

F A C T

Buyers prefer to use an agent, especially when dealing with a FSBO, because they are afraid of making a mistake. They are counting on the agent to protect them. If this is the situation, you are probably dealing with first-time buyers and there is very little you can, or should, say to dissuade them. (If you convince them *not* to use an agent and later something goes wrong with the deal, they will be very unhappy—read call a lawyer—with you.)

What Should You Do When the Buyer's Broker Wants You to Pay?

You have several alternatives. You can show the agent the door and, very possibly, say goodbye to a deal. Or you can negotiate with the agent.

Remember, in a typical real estate transaction, the buyer's broker splits the commission with the seller's broker fifty-fifty. Thus, the most you are likely to be out is a 3 percent commission.

Or you can offer the seller's agent a lesser amount. You can offer 2 percent or 1 percent or a flat fee. Remember, in real estate all commissions are negotiable.

Most likely, if it's a good agent who's worth his or her salt, they'll explain that they don't work for less than a 3 percent buyer's agent commission. With the services they offer, the work they perform, and their liability, that's the only amount they'll accept. You can either pay them what they want or they (and presumably their buyer) will go elsewhere.

But will the buyer go elsewhere? If the buyer is already in love with the property, the buyer can still come back and purchase directly through you. Or the buyer can go to another agent who is more amenable to taking a commission cut. Or the buyer can pay the agent themselves!

If you've got a buyer who's really hooked, rejecting the agent will not reject the buyer. Yes, the agent may argue powerfully to the buyer to look for another home. But if the buyer wants your home, they'll find a way to get it.

Should I Contact the Buyers Direct?

My own feeling is that you should never ask an agent to work for less then they are openly willing to work for. They may try to do a good job, but there will be underlying hard feelings throughout the transaction. And if problems arise, they will only be that more difficult to resolve.

FACT

Even if the agent originally showed the buyers the property, you are under no obligation to pay the agent a commission, unless you've signed a listing agreement. This is especially the case if the buyers first found your home on their own and signed in. In theory, they belong to you more than to any agent!

If the agent won't take less than you're willing to pay, either give up the deal and the buyer, or contact the buyer (if you know who it is) and have them seek a different agent. Yes, you may contact the buyer. There's nothing to prevent you from doing that, unless the buyers themselves prefer not to talk with you (not likely).

Explain that you're a FSBO seller. Explain how much you're willing to pay an agent (if anything) and see if you can't work something out between yourself and the buyers. Perhaps a fee-for-service agent or a discount broker will be a solution (see Chapters 4 and 5).

Discussing the commission in an open and cordial manner often results in making the deal. The buyers may be impressed with your straightforwardness and honesty. After getting to know you, they may be perfectly happy to deal with you, or not. In any event, you'll have an opportunity to strike the best commission arrangement for yourself.

Why Share (Cobroke) a Listing?

Thus far, we've been discussing a situation in which a buyer's agent comes to you with a buyer in hand. But what if the agent comes by with no buyer in hand, and instead wants to list your property on the chance they'll develop a buyer? Should you give this person a listing?

Maybe. As I said earlier, it all depends on what you want out of the deal and how much you're willing to pay to get it. A good thing to remember is that it's important not to try to reinvent the wheel. Your goal is to sell your home. You want to do it any legitimate way that you can, and if an agent can sell it with you, at less than a full commission, why not go along? Remember, the agent is not the enemy. Your true enemy is time.

If you can save time by working with an agent, it's usually to your advantage to do so. The reason is that an agent has resources that are not available to you as a FSBO seller. These include many more contacts with potential buyers than you're likely to get. Keep in mind that no matter how much effort you pour into selling your home, you're still a part-time seller. (You're probably working full-time at your regular employment.) The agent, on the other hand, presumably works full-time at selling. It stands to reason that the agent will see a lot more buyers than you will.

Further, with a shared listing, the agent can, presumably, spread the word about your home to a network of other agents. Typically, your house also will be put onto an MLS (Multiple Listing Service) so that virtually all of the agents in the area can work on it. This increases your exposure enormously and you potentially get the services of all those other agents.

FACT

It's important, however, to understand that if you give a buyer's agent a listing, you are not hiring the agent to do the selling agent's work. There are two sets of jobs—one for the buyer's agent and one for the seller's agent. In this case, *you* are agreeing to do the selling agent's work. (If you don't want to do that work, reread Chapters 4 and 5 on fee-for-service agents and discount brokers.)

What Will My Work Load Be?

This is a good time to spell it out. Here's what a selling agent normally does and what you'll need to do when acting as the selling agent, if you give out a buyer's agent listing:

- Pay for and place any advertising.
- Show the property.
- Handle your end of the negotiations with the buyer.
- Put up a sign on your property.
- Handle the paperwork.

What Will the Buyer's Agent Want Me to Sign?

Before bringing buyers to your home, the agent will want you to sign a listing agreement. The agreement should specify your relationship with the agent—what work you are expected to do, what work he or she is expected to do. It should also specify the commission you'll pay, if and when the agent produces a buyer *ready, willing, and able* to make the purchase.

There are a variety of listing agreements and we'll next look at three types available, along with an explanation of the benefits and drawbacks of each:

1. *Exclusive Right to Sell.* With this type of listing, you owe the agent a commission regardless of who sells the property, even if you sell the property entirely by yourself.

This agreement usually extends to people who see the property, even if they buy within a set time after the listing expires (often 90 days).

It's the usual agreement in a traditional listing. The idea behind it is that if the agent is paying for advertising and devoting time and effort to the sale of your property, he or she has to be assured that you won't undercut him or her by selling directly to a prospect.

2. *Exclusive Agency.* Here, the agreement is that if any agent brings in a buyer, whether it's the agent with whom you listed or any other, you have to pay a commission to your agent. However, if you find a buyer entirely on your own (meaning that buyer never contacts any agent), you don't owe the commission to anyone. This protects your agent from other agents coming in and dealing directly with you, but does not protect him or her if you find a buyer by yourself.

   This is the type of agreement sometimes used with a shared listing when you pay an up-front fee. In other words, you may pay the agent $1,000 up front whether the house sells or not. For this, the agent agrees to put the house on the MLS, put up a sign, and handle all the paperwork.

   If any agent finds a buyer, you then pay an additional fee. If you find a buyer, you're out only the original $1,000.

3. *Open Agency.* Here, you tell any and all agents who come by that you will give them a commission if they find a buyer. If they don't find a buyer, then there's no commission to pay. This arrangement has specific advantages and certain times when it can be used.

   An "open listing" is basically a nonexclusive listing. Many agents won't consider it, feeling that they might end up spending a lot of time selling a property, only to have it sold out from under them either by you or by another agent. (Note: In this listing, you pay a commission only to the agent who brings in a buyer. The agents are not required to split the commission among themselves, although they may.) The real question, however, is why would you want to give an open listing?

What Are the Differences of an Open Listing to Me?

Let's now look at it in detail. You've got your house up FSBO. You've invested in a sign, leaflets, information box, advertising, and so forth, and there you sit waiting for a buyer to come in.

Then one day, a real estate agent drives up and says that she has a client who might be interested in your home. This person has been looking for a home like yours in your price range and she would like to bring him by. However, she certainly won't bring the client over unless you're willing to pay a commission.

Because your goal is to sell your property, you tell her to go ahead, and she has you sign an open listing agreement. Basically, this says that if you sell to her buyer, you will pay her a commission. On the other hand, if you sell to someone you find or to someone brought in by another agent, you don't have to pay her anything at all.

You want to sell. Here's a potential buyer. Why not? As noted earlier, if you're smart, you'll give this agent her open listing. After all, her client might actually fall in love with the property and purchase it from you. (Note: To avoid conflicts over who initially brought whom to see the property, it is vital that you keep a list of prospective buyers who have contacted you or have already seen your house. More on this is in Chapter 11.)

By the way, with this type of listing you can't cut the agent out by calling her buyer later on suggesting that the two of you get together without the agent. A properly drawn open listing agreement is binding on the buyer for a considerable time after the property is shown.

How Much Commission Should I Agree To on an Open Listing?

You could pay as much as 6 or 7 percent. However, if you're acting as your own selling agent, 3 percent would be more ratio-

F A C T

An agent concerned that a buyer might not be loyal (might see your house and then offer to buy direct or through another agent) may ask for a one-day exclusive listing. You probably don't lose much by giving it; and you could get a sale.

nal. Remember, however, as we noted earlier, it's all negotiable. You may want to argue for a lower amount.

If an agent has a client and asks if you would give him or her an open or exclusive listing, why not say, "Sure, and I'll split the commission with you the same way as is commonly done in this area." If the going rate happens to be 5 percent and it's a 50/50 split, that means that you'll give the agent 2½ percent, if the client pans out and makes the deal.

Watch Out for the Prospect Ploy

Real estate agents know that every FSBO is a potential listing. Although it is unethical for them to do so and the vast majority will not, an unscrupulous agent may call pretending to have a buyer and solicit an open listing from you. The agent may then trot someone through your property who could be a brother-in-law or a friend. (How do you know who the client is?)

The point of this little charade is to get close to you. Once you've given an agent an open listing, for example, and that agent has brought a client by, even if the client does not purchase your home, you might be more inclined to deal with the agent. In short, the ploy could result in the agent getting a more traditional listing from you down the road.

One way to handle this is to offer to split the commission with the agent on a one-day open listing (as described above). In other words, the listing is only for the one time the agent shows the property to this very interested client. This says in a most dramatic way that you're not interested in playing games. If the agent does indeed have a legitimate client, he or she should be willing to cooperate with you for half the commission on this one buyer and no other. After all, it's the sale that counts.

If the agent is only playing games, a one-day half commission offer will often make it not worth the time to go through the phony client routine.

What Do I Do about "Listers?"

Unfortunately, many FSBO sellers are so pestered by agents that as a result, they won't even talk to them, let alone agree to give them an open listing. Some will even hang a small sign on their For Sale sign that says, "Principals Only" or "No Agents."

This is a serious mistake because it hurts you. Remember that your goal is to sell the home. The more people working toward that goal, the better. Keeping agents away, in most cases, will only delay the sale of your property.

My suggestion is that you hang a smaller sign on your property that reads, "Will Co-op with Brokers." This tells agents two things. The first is that if they have a client, you will give them at the least an open listing presumably for a part commission. (Agents are well aware of this arrangement and if they come by, will probably be ready to accept it.) Thus, they don't see you as an adversary, but as a possible source of a commission. They will want to work with you.

Second, it puts them on notice that you are serious about handling the sale yourself. "Cooperate" does not mean that you are willing to give them a traditional full listing. In the trade, it means that you will split the deal, including the commission, with them. In other words, you will work as an equal with any agent who has a client.

The house, in effect, is your own listing. You'll be willing to cobroke (cooperate with brokers) on it.

This shows that you know what you're doing and can earn the respect of agents. (A sign that tells agents to stay away, on the other hand, often only serves to earn their disdain.)

FIGURE 7.1   **Signs to Show Cooperation with Brokers**

> # "Will Co-Op with Brokers"
>
> # "Will Cobroker"

Further, such a sign puts agents on notice that they're going to get only a par (usually half) commission from you, not a traditional listing's full commission. Surprisingly, the above message on your sign, in my experience, results in far fewer agents pestering you and far more serious agents stopping by with clients. It may seem like a contrary thing to do, considering your goal is to sell FSBO, but if it works, why not go with it?

Should I Bump Up the Price to Cover the Commission?

This would probably be a bad move.

Many FSBO sellers use a straightforward approach to price when listing their property either for an open/half commission listing or an exclusive right-to-sell/full-commission listing. They take the price they were asking as a FSBO and then add to it the commission. That becomes their new asking price.

While it is true that the agent, who is in the business, has more contacts via the MLS, gets more potential buyers to see them, and has a better chance, statistically, of locating the right buyer than you do, it's not true that this input can be added in dollars to your sales price. The value of your home is what the market says it is and not a penny more. As many people have dramatically found out, the market value of your property does not depend on whether you are selling FSBO or listing with an agent. It's simply what the market will bear at the time you are selling.

Thus, if you add the cost of the commission to the price you were asking as a FSBO, and you had the house priced correctly to begin with, you will have just priced yourself up and out of the market. Potential buyers simply will not bother. They'll realize that there are other houses available, as good as yours, for less money, and they will buy those houses instead of yours.

The sad truth is that if you list, and your house was correctly priced as a FSBO, you'll get less money out of the deal. You simply can't add that commission to the price and still get a sale. What you gain is the sale itself.

Can I Conceal the FSBO Price?

Some sellers will offer their home at a lower-than-market price when selling FSBO (See Chapter 9 for a detailed explanation of why). However, when this does not attract buyers, for one reason or another, they will list and then bump up the price.

The problem arises when a buyer saw the house as a FSBO at one price, but did not want to buy it because no agent was involved. The buyer then later sees it listed at a higher price, and now wants to buy. However, this buyer only wants to pay the original FSBO price, even though an agent is now involved.

In a situation like this, you'll never get the buyer to pay the higher price because he or she will immediately realize that they are paying the equivalent of a commission. And unless they have been previously sold on paying a buyer's commission, they will not want to pop for it.

So unless you're in a fast-rising real estate market in which the buyer may be willing to pay a premium, you may end up compromising by offering the property for sale at or near the FSBO price and still paying a commission, as noted above.

The most futile thing to try is to have two prices at the same time, one a FSBO price and the other a listed price with an agent. The buyer who goes through the agent will always find out and will demand the lower price.

It's Time versus Price

Although we've covered it before, it bears repeating: The very worst thing you can do is to list too high. You'll simply increase the time it takes to find a buyer. Instead of a month, it may take six months or a year or more.

I have seen this happen many times. The FSBO seller adds on the commission and lists the house perhaps 3 to 6 percent above market. But buyers know the market (from having looked at all the similar homes for sale), and thus they don't choose your home.

Time goes by—a month, two, three. Eventually the seller realizes the mistake and lowers the price to where it should have been to begin with, but by now, the house is a stale item. It's been listed for so long that agents figure there's something wrong with it and don't bring buyers in. Even at a fair price, the house doesn't get the attention it deserves, and, as a result, it still doesn't sell. Often the poor seller must reduce the price to below market in order to attract attention and get a sale.

When Should I Give Up on Selling FSBO and List with an Exclusive Agent?

I always suggest that you set a time limit on selling your home FSBO. This time limit can be the most important thing you do with regards to selling.

Remember, the length of the time limit isn't important. It can be a week, a couple of months, or even a year. What's important is that after a set time has elapsed, you bite the bullet and stop trying to sell the property entirely by yourself. It is time to seek the aid of an agent under an exclusive-right-to-sell agreement.

I think it's worth a few sentences to reiterate why this is important. Once again: It's a matter of keeping your eye on the doughnut and not the hole. The goal is to sell your property. While you may have secondary goals of saving money or learning about transactions, none of that matters if your home never sells.

If you do everything right as a FSBO seller, you should be able to sell by yourself. But maybe your house just doesn't sell.

Why it doesn't sell may not matter. Maybe there's something you're not doing right—the house isn't fixed up well enough, you aren't offering the right financing, your price is too high, the market's terrible, you've got a very undesirable location. There are any number of possible reasons.

The point is, the house hasn't sold. You set the time limit when you started selling FSBO; now it's up. It's time to consult with a professional, an agent. After you've given it a fair shot on your own, you'd be doing yourself a disservice not to try a different avenue. Not listing when you've honestly tried to sell your home is like ignoring reality and putting your head ostrichlike in the sand. It's time to accept an exclusive-right-to-sell agreement to a committed agent whether it be full-service or discount.

Remember, your goal is to sell your home, not save a few bucks on the commission.

8

Dressing Your Home for Sale

If you want to sell quickly, you must have a better-looking house. You can talk until you're hoarse pointing out how much better your house will look once it gets a coat of paint, but, until it's painted, the buyers simply won't see it. Therefore, you need to dress your home to get a sale. To do this, the following should be done:

- Fix the entrance.
- Paint or replace the front door.
- Paint the outside of the house.
- Paint the inside of the house.
- Remove any furniture that crowds rooms or looks bad.
- Landscape the front yard.
- And anything else that needs attention.

Assuming that you're not trying to rehab your property, a good rule of thumb is to do those things that are inexpensive first, then work outward from there. Paint, wallpaper, flowers/ shrubs/lawn, and getting rid of debris all count. Do these simple things and it will make a world of difference to every potential buyer.

To reiterate, buyers almost universally only see what's in front of them. They believe, almost absolutely, only what they can see. For example, your home may boast an absolutely smashing entry with tile floors, wood trim, solid oak doors, marble columns, and more, but, if the floor, walls, and doors have been painted over with a dull, ugly paint, that's what the buyers see— dull paint, not the quality beneath.

Never mind explaining about the oak wood and tile and marble underneath. Ninety-nine percent of buyers won't pay any attention to it. All they'll see and remember is an ugly painted entry, and they'll probably dismiss your home from their minds as a contender for purchase.

Even worse, let's say that you've got a wonderful home inside. Everything is neat, clean, well kept, and looks good, but you didn't get around to taking good care of your lawn this year and the shrubs out front are wild because they weren't trimmed, and the paint is peeling. Many buyers won't even bother to stop and look inside! Never mind that the inside of your home is beautiful. The outside will chill them and they'll drive on, never knowing what they missed.

As I said, the rule is:

RULE FOR SHOWING YOUR HOUSE

Buyers believe what they see—they have no imagination.

That's what you have to work with. That's where you must begin when you prepare your house for showing. Therefore, your first job is to bypass the buyers' imagination and give them something straightforward and direct to look at. You must make your house appear smashing, wonderful, exciting, glamorous, even sexy, for that first impression. Don't let those buyers wonder about your place. Show it all at a glance. Make your house look so splendid that even someone with 20/100 vision will turn around to admire it. In other words, leave nothing to the buyers' imagination, because they don't have any.

What to Do First

Once you decide on the need to spruce up the place a bit to catch prospective buyers' attention, most sellers are immediately stopped by economic considerations. (By the way, sprucing up is really a minimum—you need to set a fire under buyers to get them to move, but it's a starting place for us here.) Few sellers have a lot of money to spend. Short of taking out a home equity loan, you may not be able to afford to fix up the old house the way it should look. Yes, you want to sell, but you don't want to bankrupt yourself doing it. Yes, you agree that you need to pre-pare the home for showing, but you can't afford, don't have the time, or lack the energy to do it all.

What can and should you do first?

RULE FOR PREPARING YOUR HOUSE

First do everything that's inexpensive.

Begin by concentrating on what costs little. This can be a tough concept for some people. The truth is that which makes the biggest impression often costs the least to do.

Let's take a few examples:

You decide to redo your family room. It's going to cost $3,000 for a wall of new bookshelves, $1,500 for new carpeting, and $500 for new window coverings. In short, you're looking at an expenditure of about $5,000.

But, you say to yourself, think of what I'll get when I sell. Right?

Wrong. Chances are that your work in the family room, admirable though it may be, won't get you a quicker sale or a higher price. In short, while you'll be spending time, money, and effort, you'll be getting nothing in return except satisfaction. (Remember your goal: You're not after satisfaction—you're after a sale!)

When a buyer comes in and "oohs and ahhs" about your family room, that person is really saying silently, "What an idiot that seller is to waste all that money on the family room. Of course, if I buy I'll enjoy it, but why should I pay a dime more for it?"

Or another example: Your backyard looks like a toxic dump site. So you haul in sand and topsoil, build a deck and overhang, plant shrubs and flowers, and put in a small pond with a couple of fish. In short, you transform that toxic dump site into scenic park land.

Now any buyer's going to be knocked over backward upon seeing your yard and rush to buy the property, right?

Wrong!

Ninety-nine percent of buyers love a great backyard, but won't pay ten cents more for it. It won't compel them to buy any quicker, either. They'll look at the front yard and the house and the first impression it gave, and if that's good, then they'll think about the backyard and add it in as a free plus.

In short, all that time, money, and effort spent on the backyard gets you a passing nod, but it doesn't make your house that much more salable.

I realize that this may fly in the face of what you have been told about selling, but I believe it to be the real truth. What gets a buyer's attention is that first impression and what makes a good first impression does not cost much. Indeed, good first impressions are often made by simple cosmetic changes.

Think of the old Hollywood sets. They used to have entire cities that were nothing more than breakfronts. They consisted of the front of a building held up with posts with no sides, back, or top, but when we watched the movie, the place looked authentic; it looked convincing; it made a strong, believable impression on us.

The same holds true for your house. The truth is that what you need to do is the cosmetic work. It's not expensive, and it will make a big difference in terms of getting you a quicker sale and a better price.

The Under-$500 Fix-Up

If you want to know what to do to effectively prepare your house for sale, Figure 8.1 gives you a short shopping list.

In short, for under $500 you can dramatically improve any buyer's first impression of your property. By so doing, you will automatically increase your chances of a quicker sale and a higher price.

Remember, don't rely on the buyer's imagination. You have to transform what the buyer first sees from something that's poor or mediocre to something that looks great. When that buyer walks in, he or she won't have to imagine what your house could look like if this were mowed or that were trimmed or the other were painted. It will be spelled out for him or her—no imagination required. Instead of a hard-to-read book, you'll give the buyer an easy-to-watch movie. Instead of what could be, you'll be showing what is. Instead of "Maybe," your buyer will be thinking, "Yes!"

Before moving on, a word about moving half the furniture out. You may be wondering what that's about. The truth is that buyers want spacious houses. Yet most of us make our houses look small by cluttering them with too much furniture. Of course, there are exceptions. If you've had an interior designer create your home's interior with matched furniture, carpeting, wall and window coverings, and so forth, you probably won't want to remove anything.

On the other hand, if the interior design of your home was directed, like mine, by what's in your pocketbook, you bought what furniture you could find when it was on sale. That means that your house has an eclectic style, a little of this, a little of that. You bought what you wanted, what you liked, what felt comfortable to you, what was affordable. As a result, total strangers with totally different likes and dislikes who walk through will proba-

FIGURE 8.1
The Under-$500 House Preparation

1. Mow the front lawn, water it, fertilize it, and get it to look great. Cost: $50
2. Plant new shrubs in front and trim old ones. Plant colorful flowers near the entrance. Clean the driveway and any cement paths. If the entrance walk is broken or damaged, pull it out and replace it with inexpensive stepping stones. Make the front look terrific. Cost: $250 to $300
3. Paint the front of your house. Use a good paint and a separate trim paint. Do an especially good job on the front door. Use a neutral color. Cost for paint: $50
4. Paint the inside entry of your home as well as the living room, dining room, and kitchen. Use a neutral color. Cost for paint: $50
5. Take half the furniture in your house and store it someplace else, preferably off the property. Put it in a relative's or a neighbor's garage. Cost: 0

Total cost:	
Front cleanup	$ 50
Entry fix-up	250
Front painting	50
Inside painting	50
Furniture removal	0
Total	$400

bly think that the place looks more like a den (as in animal) than a presentation. They will undoubtedly wonder about your taste, which simply means it's different from their own. Most of all, instead of remembering how spacious your place is, they'll recall it as a jumble of crowded, uncoordinated furniture.

How do you avoid this? Remove half your furniture. When the place looks too empty to you, too thinned out, too foreign, it will probably look great to buyers. Remember, buyers are visualizing how their furniture will look in your home. It's important to give them the impression that their furniture will fit.

Do First Things First

I am not suggesting that you make only inexpensive, cosmetic changes but that you do these inexpensive projects first. As time passes and no buyer materializes, you may want to move forward with more expensive, material improvements. Again, these should be eye-catching first, but they should be undertaken only after you've done the inexpensive, cosmetic stuff.

Let's take a look at another example: Helen and Peter have owned their home for seven years. They've decided to sell FSBO. Now they're preparing the property. When they first put the house up for sale, they cleaned and trimmed the front yard, and painted the outside front as well as the entry and big rooms inside. In short, they did all the cosmetic, inexpensive things.

It's been a couple of months now, and although they've had some nibbles, there hasn't been a buyer ready, willing, and able to purchase the property. The housing market isn't good in their area and there are few buyers. Helen and Peter are beginning to think that they need to do more to improve the appearance of their property. What should they do next?

My suggestion to them, and to you, is to do those things that are going to make the biggest impact on buyers, yet cost the least amount of money. Let's begin at the beginning, the front door. (Note: The following suggestions are in the order that they should be performed. I would do the first one first. Then the next, and so on. Ideally, you will have sold the house long before you get to the more expensive items at the end of the list.)

What about the Front Door?

The first thing that anyone sees about your house, at least the exterior of it, is the front door. Thus, the quality of your front door makes a first and lasting impression.

For this reason, I suggested earlier that you give the front door a good coat of paint when you were fixing up the front of your house. Now, if you intend to do more, I suggest you start here and replace the door(s).

A new front door isn't that expensive at a discount lumber store. You can get a good one in metal or fiberglass for around $300. For another $200, you can get it in wood. Add in the costs of the stain, hardware, and installation and you can have a brand-new front door for around $500.

Seem like a lot of money? It's not when you think of the impression it makes. A great-looking front door will knock the socks off potential buyers. I believe it returns far more than it costs in your ability to resell quicker and at a higher price.

What about Painting?

After you've painted the front of the house and the entry rooms and fixed up the front door, I suggest that you continue to paint the rest of the house. The next rooms to paint would be the kitchen, the guest bathroom, and the master bedroom, then all the other rooms.

Paint them from floor to ceiling and choose a neutral color. It's important that the color be a beige, white, or light color of some sort because many people are offended by stronger colors. I'd avoid blues, greens, and yellows. Yes, you may find a buyer who loves a specific color. But for each one of that kind of buyer, you'll come across 50 others who hate it. You have to play the odds and go with the most neutral colors.

By the way, if your house has an acoustical ceiling, popular in some parts of the country for the past couple of decades, and it's dirty, what do you do? Do you paint it?

You can. Except that it soaks up paint. It could cost you as much in time and money to paint an acoustical ceiling as it would to paint the entire rest of the inside as well as the outside of the house.

My suggestion is that you hire an acoustical contractor to reblow the ceilings. It isn't that expensive, often under $2,000 for an entire typical medium-sized house, provided there's no asbestos (typically found in homes built prior to 1978). And the difference it makes is striking. It will refresh your house and help make it look new again.

What about Carpeting?

Thus far, we've discussed items that are relatively inexpensive to do. Now we come to a big, expensive item, yet one that makes an enormous impression on buyers.

When you first walk into a house, office, or any new building, your eyes tend to drift down. We all tend to look at the floor. What do we see? Is your flooring bright, clean, and new looking? Or is it dirty, worn, and frayed?

If it's the latter, it will make a big difference in the buyers' minds. Never mind pointing out that the buyers can replace the carpeting. You have to show buyers what the house will look like with new carpeting, not just ask them to imagine it.

My suggestion is that, if you're pressed for money, at the least call in a professional carpet and floor cleaning service and have them do your house. Don't try to save money and do it yourself.

Professional services can make even an old, worn-out carpet look better. They can make a floor shine. And in most cases, they can do it for a couple hundred dollars. The steam ejector that you rent from the local supermarket may only pump dirt from one part of the carpet to another.

On the other hand, if you're really serious about selling and you have the money (or can take out a home equity loan), the best bet is to put new carpeting in the home. Brand-new, inexpensive carpeting looks almost as good as brand-new, expensive carpeting, and it looks a whole lot better than old carpeting, even some that's been cleaned.

How much does new carpeting cost? Be aware that it's probably a lot cheaper than you think. If you walk into big-name department stores or even major carpeting stores, you're likely to spend $20 to $40 a square yard. There's 9 square feet in a square yard, so if your home has 1,500 square feet of space that needs carpeting, you're talking about 167 square yards, which works out to around $3,500 at $20 a square yard (including taxes) to more than $7,000 at $40 a square yard. Either way, it's big bucks.

Only you needn't spend that much. Check with some real estate professionals in your area, particularly those who handle residential property management. They are always replacing carpeting in homes. Typically, they use a carpet broker.

A carpet broker buys directly from the mill and then sells directly to you. Often he or she does not have a store, but instead comes to your home to show you a limited number of samples.

Don't be put off by the small selection. Remember, you're not installing carpeting to walk on. You're putting in carpeting that will sell your house. All that you need is a neutral color (that will appeal to most people) and a good-looking weave.

The price? I have put brokered carpeting in houses I was preparing to sell that cost from $11 to $17 a square yard installed. It compared favorably with carpeting costing twice that price available through retail outlets. In short, you can save half the cost. For a 1,500-square-foot house, it might cost you only around $2,500 to install a good grade of nice-looking carpeting.

An additional word about color. The rule is that the carpeting always tends to look lighter when installed than it does when you look at a sample. When you're buying to live in the house, therefore, most people select darker carpeting. It doesn't show the dirt as much and it requires less cleaning.

On the other hand, when you're installing carpet to sell, the rule is buy lighter carpeting. I have installed nearly white carpeting in homes I was preparing to sell. I wouldn't think of living in the house myself because I'd have to take off my shoes before walking on it for fear of tracking in dirt that would show.

As a presentation, however, it makes the house look fabulous. Here's a case where you can take advantage of the buyers' lack of imagination. Buyers see the light carpeting and think how wonderful it looks, while not imagining all the problems it will cause when they have to live with it.

What about Rehabbing/Renovating?

Finally, there's the matter of spending even bigger bucks to renovate a kitchen or a bath, enlarge or add on a room, and do other similar work. Does this ever pay off?

Sometimes, but not often. Here's an example:

Jan and Jim felt that their old-fashioned kitchen detracted from their house. So they looked into replacing the cabinets and found it would cost around $7,000; a new countertop and other costs ran up the total about another $8,000. It would cost them close to $15,000 to rehabilitate their kitchen.

On the other hand, there was an alternative. Jim filled in the cracks and holes in the cabinets' surfaces, rehung the doors, and then painted them all. They had been a natural stained wood. But they were old, scuffed, and worn. Now they offered a bright, clean, painted look that was very modern. In addition, he re-painted the rest of the kitchen and put in new light fixtures, an inexpensive new countertop plus a sink and new faucets. The total cost was under $500.

Did it look as good as a totally rehabilitated kitchen? Certainly not. Did it look good enough to sell the house? Absolutely.

Of course, you want to do work that is appropriate for the neighborhood and the type of house you have. (For more information, check into my book, *Tips & Traps When Renovating Your Home,* McGraw-Hill, 2000.)

The same holds true for bathrooms and other rooms. When you're going to sell, spend the least amount that will give you a good-looking result. Often, cleaning, painting, and touching up can make whatever you're working on look quite appealing at a tenth of the cost of replacing.

One last word on additions and enlargements: Don't do them unless a house simply won't sell because it lacks something that people want. Maybe the kitchen is just too small. Or maybe there's no family room. Or maybe there's no fireplace.

Whatever the cause, to sell quicker and for a better price, you may have to add or enlarge. If that's the case, I suggest you either lower your price to the point where people will buy the property in spite of the defect, or bite the bullet and do the work.

Keep in mind, however, that adding or enlarging is the cost-liest of all enterprises. It takes dollars, time, and great effort.

What about the Backyard?

As noted earlier, I don't think much of spending money on the backyard. My feeling is that the vast majority of buyers are not swayed one way or another by a backyard. Therefore, this is the last place I would spend money.

Yes, I would pay the kid down the street $20 to mow the weeds, but no, I wouldn't spend a dime more than that.

You may be asking, What about all the attributes of a backyard such as a sundeck, overhang to offer shade, spa, pool, flower garden, and other amenities?

All of these are often more of a headache than they are worth. Let's take a swimming pool as an example. Today, to put in a decent-sized swimming pool with adequate decking and equipment could easily cost more than $25,000, but when it comes time to sell, can you get an additional $25,000 for the property?

Quite the contrary. Many buyers specify that the house they buy must not have a pool. They don't want the hassle of cleaning it and keeping up the chemicals. In short, you may lose as many buyers as you get by trying to sell a house with a pool.

But what about price? Won't buyers pay more for a house with a pool than for one without?

Marginally, yes. In parts of California, homes with pools tend to sell for perhaps $5,000 to $10,000 more, on average, when they sell, than houses without them, but that's a far cry from the $25,000 to $50,000 it costs to put in that pool. (On the other hand, in some neighborhoods a pool is almost mandatory to make your home competitive with others.)

If you have a house with a pool, make the best of it. Keep the pool spotless and well chlorinated—and hope that you find a buyer who's willing to pay extra to have it.

If you don't already have a pool, bite your tongue every time you want to mention the idea of adding one. I've owned many properties with pools and still own several today, and I can assure you that I have received very little financial benefit from them. In fact, they have always been more of a headache than they are worth.

Also, keep in mind your house's location when deciding what home improvements and upgrades to make. If you have the only house in the neighborhood with an in-ground pool, it will be tougher to get more money for the house.

The same holds true, to a lesser degree, for just about any other feature in the backyard. If you already have a spa, deck, gardens, overhang, and the like in your backyard, they will undoubtedly be additional selling pluses for the house, although I doubt that they will get you an additional dollar in price. On the other hand, if you don't have them, you would be just throwing money away to put them in.

Home Fix-Up For-Sale Checklist

We've looked at the different things you can do to prepare your home for sale. You'll find other suggestions throughout this book, such as getting the right kind of sign to put in front, but for here, let's recap and check off those that are aimed at making the property look more salable. See the checklist at the end of this chapter. It's also put together in the order in which the items should be completed. Do the least expensive, most impressive things first. Save those big-ticket, less-noticeable items for the very last.

How to Deal with Major Expense Items That Don't Show

Finally, we come to those items that cost a fortune to fix or replace, yet don't make any difference when it comes to appearance. I'm speaking of such things as the heating/air-conditioning system, the electrical/plumbing system, the roof (although depending on the type, some roofs will look bad when they get old and deteriorate), and broken foundations among others.

Often fixing, replacing, or adding these items can cost many thousands of dollars, yet doing so won't significantly alter the presentation of the property.

Should you spend the money?

Sometimes. You can't sell a home when the heating or air-conditioning system is broken. But you can sell a home with an old roof by fixing the leaks. Once you find a buyer, you can negotiate to pay *part* of the cost of a new roof or to fix the old one.

Of course, it goes without saying that you should definitely tell the buyer of any problems. If you don't, you might end up with a very angry buyer and, perhaps, even a lawsuit down the road.

However, once you explain the problem, you should then negotiate the cost of getting the problem fixed or replaced.

For example, I recently sold a home that had no air-conditioning, yet it was located in a moderately warm area. The buyer wanted air-conditioning for the summer months.

I explained that the house had been built without air and previous owners hadn't minded it. The buyer wasn't satisfied, so I dropped the price an additional $1,000. Then, the buyer was happy.

When Should You Spend the Money?

The point here is that almost always, big-ticket items are negotiable. New air-conditioning probably would have cost me $3,500, but here I negotiated a reduction for half what it would have cost me and made the buyer quite happy.

In another case, a house I was selling had a wood shingle roof that had deteriorated. It was leaking and old and needed to be replaced. A whole new roof would have cost around $10,000, but to fix just the areas that were bad with a guarantee of no leaks for a year would only have cost around $2,500.

The buyer ultimately wanted a complete new roof and wouldn't be satisfied with less. However, I explained that I was willing to spend only the $2,500 in repair work. We compromised: I gave him the $2,500, which he then applied toward the $10,000 replacement job after the sale. On the other hand, if I had gone ahead with the repair work, the buyer still wouldn't have been satisfied (because he wanted nothing less than a new roof) and I would still have had to negotiate a price concession. Not doing the work actually paid off.

In most cases, it pays not to do big-ticket items, but instead to point them out to the buyer and then negotiate an amount acceptable to all, which can be in the form of a sales price reduction. More often than not, this will be more acceptable to the buyer and will get you a quicker and even higher-priced sale.

FIGURE 8.2
House Fix-Up Checklist

LEAST EXPENSIVE/MUST DO

1. Mow the lawn and keep it mowed.

2. Replant grass in bare spots and fertilize lawn.

3. Trim all the hedges.

4. Plant hedges in bare spots.

5. Clean off driveway/remove oil stains.

6. Clean/fix front walkways.

7. Paint front of house.

8. Paint front doors.

9. Replace broken screens/windows in front.

10. Paint entry rooms (such as entry, living room, family room, etc.).

11. Remove half the furniture in the house. (Don't store it in the garage; leave it at a relative's or neighbor's home, or put it in a rental space area.)

MORE EXPENSIVE/OPTIONAL FIX-UP WORK

12. Replace the front door(s).

13. Paint the entire inside of the house.

14. Reblow or remove acoustical ceilings.

15. Clean or, if possible, replace all carpeting throughout house. Clean or, if possible, refinish all bare flooring.

16. Repaint or restain cabinets in the kitchen.

17. Replace light fixtures.

18. Repaint or restain cabinets in bathrooms.

FIGURE 8.2
House Fix-Up Checklist (Continued)

19. Add on or enlarge as a last resort.

20. Paint sides and rear outside of house.

THINGS NOT TO DO

1. Don't add a pool, spa, deck, lawn, or shrubs to the back-yard.

2. Don't enlarge or add on unless it's to correct a defect in the house.

3. Don't spend money on major fix-up jobs that don't show (such as replacing a roof or heating system).

9

Pricing It Right— The Key to Finding Buyers

If your price is too high, buyers simply will not bother to make offers. If it is too low, you'll lose money. What you need to find is just the right price—one that attracts buyers yet gets you the highest possible amount of money.

Warning: It's important to remember that most FSBOs are put on the market at a higher price than competing houses that are listed with agents. That's what keeps them from selling.

The Lame Seller

One would logically think that real estate agents would be afraid of FSBOs. After all, they represent competition. The opposite is actually true. Most agents love to see FSBOs for two reasons. The first we've already mentioned: FSBOs are typically priced higher than competing homes. Hence, wise agents sometimes encourage buyers to stop by FSBOs for comparison. Some agents even accompany their clients to FSBOs so that the prospective buyers can see for themselves, by comparison, just how good the listed deals are that the agent is offering.

The second reason is that FSBOs are an excellent source of listings. Agents know that a FSBO priced much higher than comparable homes in the area won't sell. Eventually the seller is going to get tired of showing the property and waiting endlessly for a buyer who never appears and list.

Price Is Everything (Almost)

Remember, the big reason that most FSBOs don't sell is the price. (A good lesson here is to go into the corner of the room and repeat to yourself three times: Price, Price, Price!) If you want to sell, particularly in today's market, you have to have a realistic price.

Why do most FSBO sellers set their prices too high to attract prospective buyers? The seller is often focusing on the wrong goal. What you, the seller, should be interested in most is selling your property. What often happens, however, is that a homeowner who decides to sell without an agent begins focusing on two different things: how much he or she wants for the property and how much he or she can save by not paying an agent's commission; hence, more money in the bank. The seller ends up with unrealistic expectations of getting a fabulous sale and saving money in the process. The end result is a house that's priced too high. It's higher than comparable houses are selling for and it keeps buyers from making offers.

You Must Sell Lower Than the Market

Here's a second point to remember: For most buyers, a FSBO is a less desirable home on which to make an offer than a listed property. This may seem to fly in the face of arguments that have long been given saying that buyers prefer FSBOs.

It's quite true, for example, that when you place your ad in the newspaper, the most compelling words you can write are, "By Owner." That's almost guaranteed to catch buyers' interest.

What's never mentioned, however, is *why* buyers are drawn to FSBOs. The reason, quite simply, is that they are looking for a bargain. They know that agents are unlikely to show them your house, so they want to check it out to be sure that they're not missing anything. They also realize that you're not paying a commission to an agent, and anticipate that you'll pass on the savings to them.

When they call or stop by, however, and discover that your house isn't any cheaper and, in fact, may be more expensive than others they have looked at, they will almost always drop you like a hot potato. Buyers don't really want to argue with you. If it doesn't cost any more, they'd prefer to have the insulation of dealing with an agent rather than an owner.

Furthermore, the minute they walk into your house and realize you're not offering it for less, they'll assume that the real reason you listed is to save for yourself, not for them, the commission an agent would charge. In addition, if you're asking more than the market price, buyers will believe the real reason is that you refuse to accept what the market will bear for your home.

Either way, you'll be branded as an unmotivated and difficult seller. In short, buyers won't want to deal with you. Why should they, when they can deal far more easily through an agent on a lower-priced, listed home?

Why Buyers Actually Prefer Agents

Although we've touched on it, let's stop for a moment to consider this: The real reason most buyers feel uncomfortable dealing directly with the seller is confrontation. Buyers may hate the way you've arranged the backyard, but they don't want to tell you because they're afraid they'll offend you. They won't, however, hesitate to tell an agent who is representing the owner.

They might love the floor plan and the way your kitchen has been updated, but they won't tell you for fear you'll stick to your price even more. They will tell an agent when making an offer.

They might really like your house, but they want to offer you much less than you're asking. However, they might find it hard to come right out and make that kind of offer, fearing that you'll be insulted. In short, most buyers dislike even the suggestion of a confrontation with a seller. That's why they prefer to talk to an agent.

How to Overcome Buyer's Resistance to a FSBO

Basically, when you sell FSBO, you're at a disadvantage. Given two identical houses located side by side, both offered at the same price, but one a FSBO and the other listed with an agent, the listed house will sell first every time.

Rule for Pricing

If you sell FSBO, you're presumably saving on the commission and have some room to play with. So give the buyers the price discount that they want, and you will sell your house faster and probably net more money.

The question becomes, how do you overcome the disadvantage? The quickest answer is offering a lower price. The mistake that most of those who sell FSBO make is thinking that they can keep the whole commission savings for themselves. You can't do that and realistically expect to sell the property in short order.

The Right Way to Price Your FSBO

It all comes back to goals. Is your goal to save money? Or is it to sell your property? If it's to sell your property, you have an excellent chance of succeeding as a FSBO, because you're in a position to offer it for less.

Let's consider the following example. You've investigated the area (as explained later in this chapter) and find that homes just like yours are usually listed for around $200,000. You also discover that three properties have sold in the past six months for an average price of $190,000. That means that buyers are typically purchasing for 5 percent less than the listed price.

You also discover that the average commission charged in your area is 6 percent. (As noted, the amount of commission charged by an agent is always negotiable; most run from 5 to 7 percent.) On a $190,000 sale, that amounts to $11,400. Those sellers who sold for $190,000 actually netted out $178,600.

Now, how much do you ask for your house?

Most FSBO sellers would ask at least $200,000. Many would ask a higher amount, figuring that their house, with its unique qualities (every house has unique qualities), is worth more. They hope to save the difference between what the other sellers netted and their own asking price.

$200,000	Price
−178,600	Other sellers' net
$ 21,400	Savings

The problem, of course, is that you'll never sell that property at $200,000. You won't even get offers. Buyers will choose to make offers on listed properties at that price (for the reasons we discussed), but not on your FSBO.

But what if you price your property at, say, $185,000? That's $15,000 less than the price of listed houses. Will you get offers? You bet you will. Buyers who might otherwise pass because of the inconvenience of dealing directly with a seller, all else being equal, will stand in line to deal directly with you if they can save $15,000. Of course, if you sold at $185,000, you would still net $6,400 more than comparable sellers who had listed and sold at $190,000 and paid a commission. Even if you had to accept a lower offer, say $178,600, exactly what other sellers had netted after a commission, you'd still be far ahead. Why? Because your house would sell more quickly, and time is not only money, it's also peace of mind.

Keeping Sight of the Goal

You must be absolutely clear on your goal. Are you interested in selling that house as quickly as possible so that you can get on with your life? Or are you interested only in saving money on the costs of the sale? If you are interested in a quick sale, you have the perfect opportunity with a FSBO because you can offer to sell for so much less than you can by going through an agent.

However, you may be interested in doing both, selling quickly and saving money. Again you're in a great position to do this, because you can still discount your house for, say, as much as you'd pay for half a commission and still make it attractive to buyers. It might take a bit longer to sell than it would with a deep discount, but the result could still be a successful sale.

Finding Out What Your House Is Really Worth

Now that we have the strategy in mind, let's see if we can put it into practice. Let's turn to the process of discovering just what the market for your home is.

Most of us loosely track housing values in our neighborhood. Anytime a nearby house sells, we usually try to learn the sales price. After all, that lets us know what our house might be worth.

However, for many of us, this process is selective. When we learn that a nearby house has sold for more, we add to the value of our house. However, when prices decline and a nearby house sells for less, we tend to dismiss that lower sale as market aberration. In other words, most of us add value when the market goes up but don't subtract value when the market goes down. Therein lies a trap that could keep you from selling your home.

Understanding the Market

The truth is that the market doesn't care how much you paid for your home; how much money, how many tears, and how much sweat you put into your home; how much you owe on your mortgage; or even how much your home was worth three years ago. All that the market cares about is what a buyer is ready, willing, and able to pay *right now*.

That statement can be very sobering, whether you sell with or without an agent. What it means is that your ability to sell in today's market is often linked directly to your ability to forget what you think your house is worth and instead sell for what a buyer will actually pay.

How Long Will It Take to Sell?

Another factor in determining price is time. The sooner you want to sell, the less you should ask. The longer you are willing or able to wait, the higher the price you can ask.

A broker friend of mine describes an experiment she did at a meeting of real estate brokers to help determine a home's value. At this meeting, the brokers each stood up and touted one of their homes to the others, hoping that by doing so, they might find an-other broker who had a buyer. When my friend stood up, she de-scribed a home that was listed for $250,000. When she was done, she asked the assembled brokers, over a hundred of them, "Does anyone have a buyer for this house at $250,000?" When no one re-plied, she asked, "Does anyone have a buyer at $240,000?" Again there were no responses. "What about at $230,000?" A few bro-kers raised their hands, tentatively indicating they might have cli-ents who could be interested.

"At $200,000 would any of you yourselves be interested in the house?" A lot of hands went up. The brokers themselves were interested in buying at that price.

Investment Value

What the above story illustrates is how price functions when a house is considered as an investment. Keep lowering the price and you will eventually find a buyer. I call this determining the commodity or the investment value. What it really shows is how important price is to selling.

Shelter Value

What the above example does not take into account is time. At the meeting my friend described, she was just testing to see how much she could get for that house if it were sold then and there. If the price got low enough, there were a lot of takers, homebuyers as well as brokers, who would buy figuring they could resell at a profit.

You'll always get plenty of buyers at fire sales or going-out-of-business sales, but prices have to be very low to attract them. On the other hand, if my friend had been willing to wait, she proba-bly could have gotten buyers at a higher price.

If you're willing to wait, you will eventually attract buyers who want to live in the property, not buy it for investment and a quick resale. You hope that these shelter buyers will show up, fall in love with your house, and pay more for it than an investor would. This is what I call the shelter value.

The shelter value is what a house will bring when it is for sale for a reasonable length of time, say 60 to 90 days. The shelter value is usually the highest amount you can get for your home. (That's why when you're selling FSBO you want to cater to buyers who plan to live in the property as opposed to investors who are looking to resell for a profit.) When it comes time to price your home, therefore, you'll undoubtedly want to get the highest shelter value. However, to do so takes time, and you'll have to determine how long you're willing to wait.

Remember that shelter value does not necessarily mean that you can get what you may feel your house is worth or what you have put into it. Shelter value is the highest price that you are likely to get by putting the house up for sale and then waiting for someone who wants to buy the property and live in it.

F A C T

You can usually get a higher price if you're willing to wait 60 to 90 days to sell your home. If you want to sell it immediately, you'll usually have to lower the price so it sells more for investment value than for shelter value.

How Much to Ask for Your House

Having noted the many pitfalls in determining price, let's now see just how much you can reasonably ask for your house. The estimating sheets in this chapter are designed to help you make comparisons with other similar homes that are for sale as well as with those that have recently sold. By finding similar homes for sale and sold, you'll come as close to knowing the true market value of your own home as anyone can, including brokers and appraisers.

The Comparison Method

There are many methods of determining the value of a property. Appraisers can use the cost approach, which bases price on cost of reproduction. Investment property is valued by the return on capital it makes. Yet in the final analysis, most properties are valued on the basis of comparison. Find out how much a comparable property sold for and that's the most likely value of yours. This is the method the mortgage appraisers, agents, and others involved in real estate use most often to determine the true value of a home. I suggest you use it, too.

The comparison method is really quite simple, in theory. All you do is find four or five houses just like yours in your neighborhood that sold over the past six months, determine the sales price, average it out, and that's what your house is worth.

In practice, however, the procedure is quite a bit more complicated. The central problem is that usually it's hard to find good comparables. There may be few sales in your area. Your house may be unique or there may be few models like it. Sales prices themselves may be skewed by seller financing, cash-down sales, or other considerations.

You could spend half your life trying to get the perfect comparables—or you could do it the easy way: check with a local agent. Say that you're going to sell FSBO now, but if the property doesn't sell you may list it with the agent. Most agents will be happy to help you. Ask for comparables. Using the computer software available in most offices, they can quickly punch up a list of comparable sales in your area.

You want to be sure the comparables have at least the similarities in Figure 9.1. If you can't find good comparables, then you'll have to do some fancy adjustments. If you find a house that's bigger or fancier than yours and that sold for more, you'll have to guess how much less your house is worth. If you find a tiny, mousy house, much smaller than yours, you'll have to guess how much more yours is worth.

In the end, add up all your comparables and average them out. Be sure to separate the price asked from the price sold. Sold prices, not asking prices, are the true value. Also, try not to use sales more than six months old. Those older than six months may

FIGURE 9.1
Similarities to Look For in Comparables

- Same area of town and similar age
- Same number of bedrooms and baths
- Roughly same square footage
- About same style and design (Don't mix Victorian with Ranch.)
- Roughly same amenities (Don't compare pool homes with those that don't have pools. If you have a fireplace, compare it with another home that also has a fireplace.)

not reflect current market conditions. Voilà! If you've done it correctly, you now should have a good idea of what your home is worth.

To help you, here are a couple of comparable estimating sheets (see Figures 9.2 and 9.3). You may want to duplicate them if you need more. When you get all of your comparables, you'll want to compare them.

Figure 9.4 is a master sheet on which to make your final calculations. To use the Master Comparable Evaluation Sheet, enter the sales price of comparable properties. Then, using the Comparable Estimating Sheet, add an amount for homes that are worse than yours and subtract an amount for homes that are better than yours. Average the figures and you'll have an average sales price and an average comparable price. If you've done your work scrupulously, the average comparable price should be very close to the market value of your home. Note: You also may want to know the average listing price. When you compare this to the sales price, you'll know how much of a discount buyers are currently getting.

FIGURE 9.2
Comparable Estimating Sheet (1)

Address
_____

Square footage
_____

Style
_____

Condition
_____

Bedrooms	Number _____	
Baths	Number _____	
Family room?	Yes _____	No _____
Garage?	Yes _____	No _____
2 car	Yes _____	No _____
3 car	Yes _____	No _____
Pool?	Yes _____	No _____
Spa?	Yes _____	No _____
Fireplace?	Yes _____	No _____
Hardwood floors?	Yes _____	No _____
Air-conditioning?	Yes _____	No _____
Good front yard?	Yes _____	No _____
Heavily traveled street?	Yes _____	No _____

General

Same neighborhood?	Yes _____	No _____
Same style?	Yes _____	No _____
Same size?	Yes _____	No _____
Same amenities?	Yes _____	No _____

List Price $ _____

Sales Price $ _____

FIGURE 9.3
Comparable Estimating Sheet (2)

Address
_____

Square footage
_____

Style
_____

Condition
_____

Bedrooms	Number _____	
Baths	Number _____	
Family room?	Yes _____	No _____
Garage?	Yes _____	No _____
2 car	Yes _____	No _____
3 car	Yes _____	No _____
Pool?	Yes _____	No _____
Spa?	Yes _____	No _____
Fireplace?	Yes _____	No _____
Hardwood floors?	Yes _____	No _____
Air-conditioning?	Yes _____	No _____
Good front yard?	Yes _____	No _____
Heavily traveled street?	Yes _____	No _____

General

Same neighborhood?	Yes _____	No _____
Same style?	Yes _____	No _____
Same size?	Yes _____	No _____
Same amenities?	Yes _____	No _____

List Price $ _____

Sales Price $ _____

FIGURE 9.4
Master Comparable Evaluation Sheet

	Sales Price	Add/Subtract	Comp. Price
House #1	$ _____	$ _____	$ _____
House #2	$ _____	$ _____	$ _____
House #3	$ _____	$ _____	$ _____
House #4	$ _____	$ _____	$ _____
House #5	$ _____	$ _____	$ _____
House #6	$ _____	$ _____	$ _____
House #7	$ _____	$ _____	$ _____

Average Sales Price $ _____

Average Comp Price $ _____

Advertising That Gets Results, Fast

At any given time there are probably at least a dozen potential buyers out there who would just love to purchase your home. If you could just get a list of them, you could send them letters, call them, and even wine and dine them. They would all be interested and, in a few days, chances are you would have a dozen offers.

The problem is finding just those 12. How do you distinguish them from everyone else? Consider you may be living in a town that has 25,000 people in it or a city with a million or more. How do you find from all the others just the few that will purchase your property? To get to those few people who might really be buyers for your home, you may need to wade through thousands who aren't. To put it another way, you need to get your message to as many people as possible in the hope that a few of them will be the right ones.

How do you do this? The answer is that you publicize and even advertise your property in as wide a variety of media as possible. You do whatever you can to get the word out.

This can be expensive, such as a lot of newspaper and even radio/TV advertising (which some spendthrift and desperate sellers have done in different parts of the country), or it can be inexpensive but clever. I strongly suggest going the latter route. Here are the ways you can advertise your property most effectively, yet most cheaply.

Start with a Sign

A sign on the property is the single most effective advertising tool at your command. It lets everyone in the area know your home is for sale. (After all, how else would you discover that one of your neighbors is interested in buying?) The sign also allows anyone driving down the street to learn that your home is for sale. And when you advertise and people call and ask for directions to your property, you can simply direct them to your street and when they get close, the sign will bring them home.

There is, however, a negative to putting a sign in your front yard. It lets everyone, including those with potentially criminal intent, know that you are trying to sell. Quite frankly, some people out there look for FSBO houses and then call the owners, purporting to be interested in buying, when their real intent is to scout out the property for a potential robbery. Your best defense here is to carefully screen any potential buyers. Please see Chapter 12 for tips on that.

Can I Build My Own Sign?

Anyone can put together a sign, but it takes a bit of knowledge to build a sign that's effective and snares potential buyers instead of shying them away. Here's what to watch for.

To begin, don't buy a ready-made sign at the store for a couple of dollars that says "For Sale By Owner" and gives you a place in which to write in your phone number (see Figure 10.1).

These cheap, ready-made signs look just that, cheap. Potential buyers driving by are likely to think that you are a rank amateur, may not be very serious, and probably don't know much about what you are doing. After all, if you're not even willing to get a decent sign, how committed are you actually to selling the property?

FIGURE 10.1   FSBO Sign to Avoid

Get a professionally made sign. These may cost you $50 or so, but they look good, catch attention, and say that you're a committed seller and know what you're doing.

How do you know a good sign? It will look just like an agent's sign. It will be roughly the same size (20 inches by 30 inches), the lettering will be clear and in a color readily seen, such as red, and it will be well designed and not look amateurish. The sign should also contain vital information.

Where Do I Put the Sign?

Placement of the sign is important. It should be clearly visible from cars traveling both ways on the street. If necessary, particularly for corner lots, you may need to post separate signs, one at each end of the property. Often, you may want to have two signs back-to-back placed in the front of your property.

A sign parallel to the house might be difficult to see except when someone is right in front. A double sign placed perpendicular to the house can be read easily by people in cars as they drive by.

A word of caution: Some cities restrict the kind of sign you may put on your home. Check with your local zoning department. Many condominium associations prohibit owners from putting signs in their front yard. You may be limited, in this case, to a small sign in a window.

FIGURE 10.2
Information to Place on a FSBO Sign

FOR SALE
Builders, landscapers, and politicians put signs in yards. You want people to know that in your case, it's the house that's for sale. These words and your phone number should be the largest elements.

BY OWNER
This may be your best selling point. It doesn't have to be large, but it should be prominent.

BEDS/BATHS
I always suggest that you list how many bedrooms and bathrooms your house has. Many buyers are looking for certain sizes. For example, yours may be a four-bedroom, three-bath house. This is a plus. (If you have only two bedrooms—a minus—you may want to leave this fact off the sign.)

ONE SPECIAL FEATURE
You don't really have room for more than one. Typically you might say "Pool" or "Spa" or "Large Yard." Often this can be attached as a separate, smaller part of the sign.

SHOWN BY APPOINTMENT
This is an important part of your sign. Without it, you will have people knocking at your door constantly. You may still have some of these. But, hopefully, most people will call first and you can screen them before admitting them to your home.

PHONE NUMBER
This must be large and clear. Use sans serif type. It's easiest to read.

Use an Information Box

The sign is an attention-getter, but by itself, it isn't going to hook a prospect. It may cause them to slow down, look at your home, and jot down the phone number. The problem is that they

FIGURE 10.3   More Effective FSBO Sign

may not have a pen handy or a piece of paper, or the whole thing may seem like too much hassle at the time.

A prospect needs more information than is on the sign to determine if this is a house to be considered. Thus, many good agents have taken to hanging an information box just below the For Sale sign. The information box contains copies of a leaflet that gives much more detailed information on the property (see Figure 10.5). It answers some of the potential buyers' questions as well as whets their appetites to see the house. The leaflet is actually a great marketing tool and I urge you to use it.

You can easily build the information box yourself. All that you need is a small wood or metal box that will shed water and keep direct sunlight away. (The sunlight tends to fade whatever's written on your leaflets.) Hang the box on the post holding the sign and label it "For More Information" or "Free Leaflet" or "Free, Take One."

Potential buyers will get the idea. They'll stop the car, get out, and pick up the leaflet. Instantly they have a host of information about your home.

It's a good idea to be careful about what you put in and leave out of the leaflet. It may be the very item that will make a buyer really enthusiastic about your property. If this sheet is done prop-

FIGURE 10.4 Sample Information Box

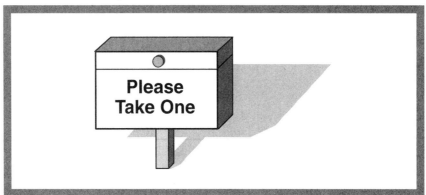

erly, it will give all the information a buyer really needs to decide that your home is one that he or she may want to look at further.

Be careful—you don't want to include too much information. For example, never include specific financial information such as your existing mortgages. Don't put down what you originally paid for the property. These sorts of things may come up later, but they shouldn't be the first thing that a buyer sees. Be sure all information is accurate.

Always include a photo of your house. The old adage "a picture is worth a thousand words" applies here. Just being able to see your house often will allow a potential buyer to determine whether your place is in the running. You don't have to be a professional photographer (or hire one) to take the picture. Any point-and-shoot camera will do. Try to take the picture on a day that is overcast. The house will come out quite clearly. If you take the shot in bright sunlight, you'll end up with too many shadows.

The information leaflet won't cost a lot to produce. You can handle the typing yourself and get the sheet reproduced for about a nickel a page at most copy centers. A 4-inch by 6-inch photo is more expensive, but it still can be reproduced for between a quarter and half a dollar apiece if ordered in quantities.

FIGURE 10.5
What to Put in the Leaflet in Your Info Box

Buyer's guide to (address goes here) _____

Price _____

Contact _____

Grammar school _____

Intermediate school _____

High school _____

# of Bedrooms _____

# of Baths _____

Size of garage (1-, 2- or 3-car)

Air-conditioning? _____

Pool or spa? _____

Lot size _____ $\times$ _____

Age _____

Special features _____

Photo (color, if possible) of your house

Your phone number (large) goes here _____

Don't Keep It a Secret

Once you've got this leaflet, it would be a shame not to go around and pin it up at a wide variety of other places where potential buyers might stop by. Some suggestions include:

- *Housing offices.* Schools, military installations, and larger corporations often operate housing offices for their people to help them find places to live. Often these people are looking to buy. I suggest that you contact any place near your home (within a 10-to 15-mile radius) and ask the staff if you can hang your leaflet in the office. Most of the time, they will be happy to have you do this. (While you can call and then send in the leaflet, my suggestion is that you actually stop by. That way you'll know that it gets hung up.)

- *Bulletin boards.* Shopping centers, stores, libraries, civic centers, public buildings, and other areas often have a public bulletin board. Don't be shy about hanging your leaflet. Just keep in mind that you will have to go back every couple of weeks to be sure it's still hanging there. (Sometimes it's a good idea to attach a half dozen small Post-its to the bottom of your sheet with your address and phone number so that anyone interested can take this information. Otherwise, they will tend simply to rip down the leaflet.)

What about Newspaper Ads?

Free publicity is what we've considered thus far, getting the information out for no cost. (Yes, it will cost you for a sign and a leaflet, but after that the publicity doesn't cost anything.)

Unfortunately, to reach the largest number of people in a reasonable amount of time, you probably have to go one step better: paid advertising. This usually takes the form of your local newspaper.

The trouble with newspaper ads is that they are so expensive. If your paper has even a modest circulation, it can easily cost $25 a week for a tiny ad and much more for an ad in which you can elaborate on your home. Nevertheless, to get the word out, you can't afford to miss this important medium.

My suggestion is that you try both kinds of ads, the little inexpensive ones and the bigger, more descriptive ads. (We'll look at examples of both shortly.) You may want to alternate ads on different weeks. One word of caution: Never run the same ad for more than a week. When potential buyers see the same ad run over a longer period of time, they begin to recognize it and often think of it as that house that still hasn't sold. You don't want readers to think of your house as stale on the market, but as fresh. Hence, my suggestion is that you create a number of different ads and rotate them.

Also, you may find that you have a choice of where to place your ad. In my community, there are one major and two local paid newspapers plus at least three flyers that are delivered free

FIGURE 10.6
The Basics to Cover in an Ad

1. FSBO—Usually this means the ad starts with the words "By Owner."

2. Price—Buyers shop by price. If your house is $200,000, you're wasting your time with buyers who are looking for $100,000 or $300,000 homes.

3. Location—Buyers within a price range always shop location. You needn't give out your street address. Just give the tract or the area of town.

4. Size—Typically this means the number of bedrooms and bathrooms.

5. Best Selling Feature—This could be a large lot or a pool/spa, the fact that it's redecorated or has an extra room, or some other attribute.

6. Inducements—Here I mean words indicating that you are eager to sell or that this is an especially good buy or some other reason that will motivate a buyer to call.

7. Phone Number—Forget this and the ad's a waste.

around town. All accept paid advertising. Obviously, I can't advertise in all six, as it would be prohibitively expensive.

Therefore, I suggest that you do what I do, which is to borrow the marketing savvy of those whose business it is to know which papers get the most attention. I get a couple of copies of each and then see which ones carry the most real estate advertising, particularly advertising by agents whose livelihood depends on knowing how to get the most out of their advertising dollar. Typically, one or maybe two newspapers or flyers will carry a significantly larger number of ads for homes than the others. That's the one I would use for my own ad and I suggest you do likewise. Of course, if after a couple of tries you get poor results, you can always switch to a different paper.

FIGURE 10.7   A Short but Effective Ad

BY OWNER

$205,000, split-level, Shadow Hills, 4 + 3 Pool, Large lot, anxious, make offer 555-9087

Try Small Ads

The small ad has only the most meager ingredients. It usually reads as one long sentence and is often heavily abbreviated. (The ad itself can vary enormously, but you're simply not going to get a whole lot into just three to five lines.)

As long as you include the following basics, you've done your best:

- FSBO
- Price
- Location
- Size
- Best feature(s)
- Inducement
- Phone number

By the way, many sellers, particularly those old-timers who have done this many times, swear by this small ad. They say that real buyers comb the newspapers and look especially for the tiny ads by owner. They claim that these small ads often get twice the response of much larger ads. My own experience tends to confirm this.

One final word about the lead. The expression "For Sale By Owner" is one of the biggest selling features. Buyers know that they may have already seen properties advertised by agents (because of their cooperation through listing services). However, if it's by owner, unless they've been by your house, chances are they haven't seen it.

Of course, you may want to switch and stick the most important feature as the lead. It could be the size, the location, the fea-

FIGURE 10.8
What Makes Your Home More Saleable?

- Good price
- Owner-assisted financing/Low down/Low payments
- Great location
- Larger size than . . .
- More room (bigger lot, more bedrooms)
- Unusual features

tures, anything. Just be sure that somewhere in the ad you also include the fact that you're selling FSBO.

Try Larger Ads

As your ad gets larger (and more expensive), you can afford to expand on the features of what you're selling. However, you want to be sure that you don't waste space (and money). What you say should be the most powerful inducement possible to snag buyers.

To accomplish this, I suggest you limit each ad to a single, positive theme; that is, to point out how your house is different, and a better deal, than other homes on the market. You have to identify what makes your home outstanding.

Writing an Ad That Pulls

Large corporations spend billions of dollars annually to come up with catchy advertising that will sell products. So you may think, what chance do you have of writing a winning ad for your home?

Your chances, actually, are excellent. The reason is that you don't need to create an advertising campaign or write a hundred words of great copy. You need only two or three good ads to alternate in the newspaper. Further, you can save a couple of Sunday papers (when the real estate advertising is heavy), note those

FIGURE 10.9   Sample Price Ad

REDUCED!

For quick sale—Split-level with fireplace, great area close to top schools, manicured lot, recently painted, new carpeting, 4 + 2 with FR. Make offer and move in before summer's over! By owner. $189,950, 555-2345.

ads by agents that catch your attention, and build your ad around them. They say that copying is the sincerest form of flattery, and while I don't suggest you copy someone else's ad verbatim, you can borrow the idea without any problem. Another bit of wisdom is that there's nothing new under the sun, which means that the ads you see were probably themselves based on and taken from other advertising.

As noted above, it is important to get across the main theme in your ad. Therefore, I've included a number of ideas, all of which are based on actual ads taken from several newspapers over a period of a few weeks. By the way, you may want to vary the theme of your ad from week to week. If you find that pushing the size of your property doesn't work, you may want to push the low down payment or reduced price. At different times, buyers respond to different incentives (depending on the economy, market conditions, what's available, etc.).

Feature Price

The incentive here is that your price is lower in some way. If you can say that yours is the lowest-priced three-bedroom, two-bath home in your area, it's a great come-on. Just be sure it's true. A safer tactic can be to advertise your price outright or, as in Figure 10.9, emphasize that your price is lower than it was before.

Of course, also keep in mind that while your theme is what may catch a reader's eye, it's all of the other features that will convince that reader to make the call. Figure 10.10 is another example of a price ad.

FIGURE 10.10   Another Sample Price Ad

> ### SELLER DESPERATE!
>
> Must sell, make offer. Top location, four large bedrooms with bonus room over garage. Formal dining room with wet bar in den. Lender is threatening, see now. $279,950 by owner. 555-2211.

Feature a Low Down Payment or Better Financing

Here your goal is to attract buyers who don't have enough cash to purchase a house in the normal way. Your advertising must emphasize the financial aspects. The buyer can get in with a lower-than-normal down payment, lower monthly payments, or greater ease in qualifying for a mortgage.

Remember, always put the theme of your ad into the lead. The first line, or lead, is what catches attention. If it's something that readers want, they will read on with interest. Otherwise, they'll just skim past it. Also remember that each time you emphasize one aspect of your property or financing, you downplay another. If you point out the wonderfully low down payment, as shown, a buyer with enough money down, but who needs easy qualifying for a mortgage, may skip right over it. That's why I suggest several ads that run on alternating weeks, each emphasizing a different theme.

Note that when you're advertising the financing, sometimes it isn't necessary to include the exact price. After all, a potential buyer has all the necessary information in this ad, if he or she is looking for easy qualifying (assumability, interest rate, and monthly payment). Often, a fully assumable loan at a good interest rate will allow the seller to get a better price, assuming that it's an unusual situation for the market.

Be careful of advertising something that is commonly available. In the Phoenix market, for example, virtually every other inexpensive house used to have an assumable loan, so emphasizing that didn't impress too many buyers.

FIGURE 10.11   Sample Low Down Payment Ad

LOW DOWN PAYMENT!

Only $3,000 moves you in! Seller will carry 15 percent second at reduced interest rate. Hurry, won't last long. Two-bed adult condo, $97K by owner, 555-5123.

Feature Your Amenities Ad

In some areas and in some markets, it's not price or down payment that sells; it's what the house itself has to offer. This is particularly the case if your home is in a more exclusive area.

Here the owner is emphasizing all the special amenities of the house. Presumably, buyers in this price range are looking for features, rather than terms and price. (This isn't always the case; most of the time buyers are concerned about price and terms as well. But all things being equal, amenities will sell.)

The ad in Figure 10.13 was taken from a paper near San Francisco (where prices are among the highest in the country). While the house must be nice, the advertisement actually wastes the owner's money. In this price range and suburb one would expect hardwood floors, air-conditioning, three-car garage, and good location. Mentioning this isn't going to impress the reader.

Further, the phrase "must see to appreciate" is frequently found in real estate agent ads and is often used to describe a property that's really in a poor location. Hence, repeating it here is likely to make potential buyers wary. The ad would do far better to emphasize features truly exclusive to this house.

FIGURE 10.12   Sample Financing Ad

ASSUMABLE LOAN!

FHA fully assumable 6½%. Pmts. only $1,337 per month. Seller will consider financing part of down. Choice location; must sell by April 1 or lose! Come see, make offer today. By owner, 555-6789.

FIGURE 10.13 Sample Features Ad That Doesn't Work

EXECUTIVE MANSION!

Big 5 + 4 with lighted tennis court. Solid wood oak floors throughout, air, 2-story, pool with spa, garden-like setting, secluded, 3-car garage, choice location, has it all—must see to appreciate $655K, For Sale By Owner, 555-5551.

The ad in Figure 10.14 has fewer lines than the one preceding it, yet it has more of the specifics that appeal to the kind of buyer the seller wants to attract. The rule here is that when in doubt, be as specific as possible.

One point to reemphasize: Don't put the address in the ad. The address not only lets potential buyers know where the house is; it also lets those with robbery on their minds know. Let the buyers call. Screen them on the phone. Then arrange for a time to show the property when you know you'll be there. More about this is discussed in Chapters 11 and 12.

Feature Size

Sometimes what makes your house special is its size, or the size of the lot. If so, you need to get that information to the reader. Once again, however, remember that you may have the biggest house or lot in town, but if the price and terms are wrong, it probably still won't sell. Just having a big yard or home isn't by itself necessarily all that wonderful.

FIGURE 10.14 Sample Features Ad That Does Work

EXECUTIVE MANSION!

Huge 5 + 4 with two-story view of Mt. Diablo, wine cellar, pool/spa, lighted tennis court, secluded, in-town location, one-of-a-kind $655K, For Sale By Owner, 555-5551.

FIGURE 10.15   Another Sample Features Ad that Doesn't Work

ROOM TO ROAM

A full ⅓ acre with 11 mature fruit trees. Zoned for horse lover, includes barn with new roof. Low maintenance/low water irrigation system. Ranch house with in/out gas barbecue, over 2,600 usable ft. of space. Circular drive and more. $319,950, FSBO. Call 555-5432.

In an ad taken from a Los Angeles paper, the seller is pointing out that the one-third acre has fruit trees and a barn, in case a horse owner is looking for property. In other words, it isn't just space, but is usable space.

The drawback here is that one-third acre is probably too small for horse raising and fruit trees, and this fact won't be lost on a potential buyer. You can't really advertise that you have room for horses unless you are selling a pasture.

The Unusual Feature Ad

Finally, there's the ad that offers a special feature. It could be an indoor grill, an added-on playroom, a special décor, or, as in Figure 10.16, the location of the property.

Caution: Many owners feel that their property is well located when, compared with other properties, it isn't. My suggestion is that you ask several agents to name the best feature of your home. They can often point out whether it's really location or something else.

Advertising Elsewhere

A variety of other avenues of advertising may be open to you. A promising new medium is cable television. Most cable systems have a public access channel that is open to a wide variety of local programming.

FIGURE 10.16   **Unusual Feature Ad**

> ### LOCATION, LOCATION, LOCATION!
>
> It's everything and this home has it all located next to top shopping and transportation in the heart of the desirable Westlake area. 3 + 2 with wet bar, spa, and RV parking. $190K by owner. Call 555-1122.

Often they will run a commercial for a product, say your house, for a nominal fee to cover setup costs. The fees are typically under $50 and often around $25. You can prepare a short commercial, of about 30 seconds, using a home camcorder. You can show the front, back, and inside of your home as well as describe the price, terms, and attributes. (It's really amazing what you can get into a 30-second slot.)

I urge you to try this avenue. Keep in mind that the only people who are likely to watch and listen to this sort of commercial are buyers, but, after all, who are you looking to attract?

Talking Up Your House

Finally, there's the old tried-and-true method of talking up your property. How many people do you come in contact with in a day, a week? If you're working and socially active, the number could actually be in the hundreds. My suggestion is that you bring up the subject of your home for sale with everyone you meet. Talk to your coworkers, especially your neighbors, the lunch counter cook, your friends, everyone and anyone.

You never know who's looking to buy a house. A few of the people to whom you talk, if they aren't in the market themselves, may know others who are. Think of it as starting a rumor. It expands as it goes, reaching more and more people. Eventually, it may catch the ear of just the right buyer for your home.

FIGURE 10.17
Getting the Word Out Worksheet

1. Sign (visible from both directions)

2. Information box

3. Information leaflet (or pass out)

4. Distribute leaflet at:
   Housing offices
   Bulletin boards
   Shopping centers
   Malls
   Schools

5. Short newspaper ads

6. Longer ads

7. Online

Worksheet for Finding Prospects

The worksheet in Figure 10.17 is intended both as a review and a checklist. It gives you the potential sources for finding prospects for your FSBO. You aren't finished advertising your property until you've got a check in each column. Don't forget the less formal technique of informing friends, relatives, and coworkers that your house is for sale.

11

Hooking a Buyer

Do you feel comfortable about selling something as big as a house?

You should. It's simply a matter of showing off a product that you already know inside and out.

All you have to do is to get the buyer to trust you. Establish a working relationship and the rest will take care of itself, right up through the signing of the sales agreement.

How Do I Establish a Working Relationship with the Buyer?

As the seller of a home dealing directly with a buyer, you are suspect. The buyer suspects that you will do anything and everything to sell that home, including lying and cheating. The buyer sees you as the adversary. Therefore, if you're going to deal effectively with that buyer and come to terms that are acceptable in a successful sale, you have to establish trust.

How do you do that?

The way to win trust is to be trustworthy. It sounds simple, yet is complicated. The four rules for winning the trust of the buyer are:

1. Never personally offend the buyer.
2. Never hide a defect in your property.
3. Never lie about anything involving the sale.
4. Never offer to do something you can't do.

1. Never Offend the Buyer

This is far easier to say than to do. Basically, you must keep things strictly on a business level. If the buyer says that your favorite rose bush looks like a weed, you don't have to agree. But you also don't have to disagree. You can simply point out that roses come in all shapes and sizes.

If the buyer notes that the color you've painted the stones over your fireplace is hideous, you don't have to get agitated and protest that florid pink goes great over river stones. Simply nod, acknowledging the buyer's opinion, and move on.

The point is simple. As soon as you do anything to offend the buyer, you turn a business deal into a personal disagreement, and no one wants to deal with someone he or she doesn't like. Offend the buyer and you could lose a deal.

2. Never Hide a Defect

Chances are that if you attempt to hide a defect, it will come out sooner or later. For example, you seal and paint some cracks in the walls that are caused by a broken foundation. As soon as the buyer notices the bad foundation and hidden cracks or finds them through an inspection, he or she will distrust you. A buyer who might otherwise be willing to go ahead with the sale if the foundation is fixed, or if there is an adjustment in price, will now wonder what else you've concealed.

A buyer who distrusts you won't want to deal with you and the sale may be lost.

3. Never Lie About the Property or the Deal

You state that the roof is perfect; it never leaks. But the buyer discovers moisture in the attic. You attempt to cover your tracks by saying it's just condensation or maybe a leaking pipe.

Then the buyer notices light peeking through between shingles and concludes that you're a liar, not to be trusted or dealt with. A potential deal could be lost.

4. Never Say You'll Do Something You Can't Do

You say that you know all about real estate financing, and you'll help the buyer get a loan. You promise that the buyer can qualify for a 95 percent loan, but, after he or she agrees to buy, you both discover that the maximum loan the buyer can get is 80 percent. The buyer can't complete the purchase as negotiated and, feeling cheated, won't come up with more money. The deal may be lost.

In short, always be courteous, reasonable, and truthful. If you do, the buyer will soon see that you are someone with whom he or she can work with and who can be counted on—and someone he or she will want to deal with. If you don't, you'll find that distrust sours every buyer with whom you deal. Remember, if you try to hide something or lie, little inconsistencies will do you in. Buyers, who are naturally suspicious, are looking for those inconsistencies. Honesty is the key to establishing a relationship with the buyer. The buyer doesn't have to like you (although that does help), but must respect you if the two of you are to conclude a successful real estate sale.

Putting Your Salesmanship to the Test

I've always maintained that the product, in this case the house, either sells itself or it doesn't. Thus, assuming you've fixed up your property as described in Chapter 8, when it comes to selling, your job is largely informational. You need to be sure that the potential prospect is informed of all of the features and advantages of the home.

This doesn't mean that you spend a lot of time talking off the prospect's ear. Often, a sale can be lost because the salesperson talks so much that the potential buyer never gets a chance to really see the house and finally leaves rather than listen anymore.

What's needed is getting prospects in, letting them look around, and being ready to answer any questions. We'll have more to say about this shortly. First, let's consider just how to deal with prospects at first contact, which usually means the initial phone call.

Answering the Phone

It's important at the outset, vital even, to understand that when you're selling your home, it's at the buyer's convenience, not yours. I think the analogy of fishing is helpful: When you go fishing, it's not the fish's responsibility to get on your hook; it's up to you to have that hook in the water, properly baited, and waiting for as long as it takes to get a nibble.

The same holds true for selling your home. It's not the buyer's responsibility to keep calling you repeatedly until he or she finally finds you at home. It's up to you to be sure that every phone call is promptly answered, that information is provided, and that you at least get the caller's name and phone number.

What this means is that as soon as you put your house up for sale by owner with your phone number on your sign, leaflets, and advertising, your phone must never be unattended. It's going to take a little extra effort and, perhaps, a couple of bucks, but being sure that the phone is always answered is the first step in hooking a buyer. Ideally, you would be home 24 hours a day, ready to answer any buyer's questions. Obviously, that's not going to happen. So what's next best?

Use a Cell Phone

Cell phones are inexpensive and their beauty is that the caller never really knows where he or she is calling. You could be at home, or in a car, or out shopping, or almost anywhere. When that prospect calls, you're there to answer.

The downside is that often when that prospect calls, you're not in a good position to write down important information, like a callback number. This is especially the case if you're in your car. It's awkward to ask the caller to call back and leave their phone number. Indeed, you can figure it just won't happen. (Some cell phones offer an automatic call-back feature.)

FIGURE 11.1
Typical Answering Machine Message

"You've reached the Smith home. Yes, it's for sale and, yes, we'd love to show it to you. The price is $195,000, we offer excellent seller financing, the house is large with four bedrooms and two baths and is recently redecorated. Please leave your name and number and we'll call you back as soon as possible to make an appointment to show it."

Nevertheless, for immediacy there's nothing as good as a cell phone. You can be on it 24/7.

Use an Answering Machine

On the other hand, there are distinct advantages to using an answering machine. An answering machine with the proper message can cover for you. Further, you're more likely to get a number to call back with the answering machine. I suggest that you use a message like the one in Figure 11.1.

I can recite this message easily within 15 seconds, which is the time most answering machines provide for outgoing messages. The message itself tends to be buoyant and informative, and has just enough of a hook to get potential buyers to leave their names and phone numbers.

A word of caution: Because one of your goals is to get the caller's name and number, some sellers are inclined to use only an answering machine. That way, they feel they are sure to get that caller's name and number even before they begin a conversation.

Bad move.

Many buyers, sincere buyers, won't leave a name and number. They don't want to be bothered by sellers who may be desperate and may make pests of themselves by repeatedly calling back. The answering machine is only second best to answering the call yourself. Use it only if you can't be there or if using a cell phone is impractical.

Note: You can use *both* an answering machine and a cell phone. Use your home phone line as your basic incoming phone number for ads. Then do one of the three following:

1. Answer the call yourself from home.
2. Use call forwarding to have it forwarded to your cell phone.
3. Use an answering machine (either at home or on your cell phone).

A Designated Answerer

The least desirable alternative, to my way of thinking, is having another family member answer the phone. Sometimes this is inevitable, as when a potential buyer or seller calls in the evening and your son or daughter picks up the phone.

F A C T

You may be able to get your caller's phone number without even asking, if you use "caller ID" and the person phoning doesn't have their number blocked.

Be sure to cue everyone that if a call is about the house, it should go to you immediately. If you're not there, instruct whoever answers the phone to get only the name and number for you to call back. If another person begins giving out information about your house, the person may blow it, presenting the information in such a way that a buyer gets turned off or decides too hastily that this place is not for him or her.

The worst scenario is a child answering the phone. Even a teenager may turn the buyer off unless he or she is very comfortable responding to phone calls and knows exactly what to say.

The best situation is to have a designated answerer—you, your spouse, or someone else. If a buyer calls and anyone else picks up the phone, the caller should be quickly transferred to that designated person. If the designated answerer isn't home,

---

FIGURE 11.2
The Phone Report

1. What is your name? _____

2. What is your home phone number? _____

3. What is your work phone number in case I can't catch you at home? _____

4. Are you a local resident? _____

5. Where do you live? (What part of town?) _____

_____

6. Are you from out of town? _____

7. Where are you staying locally? _____

8. Do you currently own a house?_____ opt.

9. Is your current house sold?_____ opt.

10. Is it listed or FSBO?_____ opt.

11. When do you plan to sell and move? _____ opt.

12. What is your monthly or annual income?_____ opt.

---

whoever answered should take a simple message—name and phone number. It's clear-cut and leaves little room for error.

A Dedicated Phone Line

Finally, consider putting in a separate phone line during the time you have your home for sale. The line would be dedicated strictly to calls on the house. All of your advertising (sign, leaflets, etc.) would give that number only. When that dedicated phone line rings, you know that it is someone inquiring about the house.

Yes, a separate line costs a few dollars more, but if you're really sincere about selling your house, it could be well worth the added expense.

Use a Phone Report

The purpose of the phone report shown in Figure 11.2 is threefold. First, it identifies the caller and gives you his or her phone number plus other information to help you determine if you want to show your home to this person. (When you are selling FSBO, your security must always be a consideration—see Chapter 12 for more on this.) Second, getting the phone number means that you can call the party back at a later date to ask how the house hunting is coming along and perhaps rekindle interest in your place. Third, it is the first step in helping you to qualify a potential buyer. After you've talked for a while, the buyer may provide enough information for you to determine whether he or she has sufficient income and strong enough credit to purchase your home.

Asking Questions

It's important to understand that when a potential buyer calls you, don't begin the conversation by asking the questions on the phone report (although a family member who's taking a message might do just that with at least the caller's name and phone number). When you, the seller, get a phone response to an ad, your sign, or some other source, you should first describe your home.

Describe how it looks, how big it is, how good the location is, and so forth. You should give the potential buyer information. I don't mean that you should just jabber on and on. Listen carefully to what the caller says and try to answer questions honestly and completely.

For the buyers, the first part of the conversation is always a matter of determining whether your house is even remotely close to what they are looking for. Buyers will ask about the price, size, special terms, and, most important, location. If the conversation goes on for a while and the buyer seems interested, then you can offer to show the house. If the caller agrees, then you are perfectly within your rights to ask for a name, phone number, and other such information. I suggest that the questions be asked informally, as if you're just curious (which you are), not as if you're an inquisitor.

The first seven questions listed in the phone report are pretty straightforward, and most potential buyers won't usually hesitate to answer them. After all, if they're going to come and see your house, they can understand your interest in learning a little bit about them. Questions 8 through 12 are a bit trickier. They involve specific questions that will help you determine if this is a real buyer with whom you should spend time or just a prospect.

If the caller already owns a house he or she is living in, hasn't sold it, and hasn't even put it up for sale, you're not dealing with a buyer. This person is perhaps months away from being able to buy. You may want to get the number and call back a couple of months later (if your house is still for sale) to see if he or she is closer to selling the current home.

Question 12 is the trickiest of all. This information is important to you because it tells you pretty closely whether the caller can qualify to purchase your home. The trouble is that most people aren't willing to disclose this information, at least over the phone. My suggestion is that you don't ask this question at all unless you've established a good rapport with the caller. Then, ask it only if the subject of qualifying for your home comes up in the course of conversation.

For example, the caller might say something such as, "Your price seems rather high. I don't know if we can afford that much." To which you might reply, "Well, how much do you make? I can quickly tell you if it's enough for a loan." And so forth.

Keep one thing in mind: Because you're a FSBO seller, the caller is going to be just a bit wary of confiding too much in you. After all, you're the person that caller is going to have to negotiate with if he or she decides to buy. Therefore, don't push too hard. If the caller hesitates and doesn't want to answer, let it go.

The Bottom Line

If you've done your homework, you will quickly find that your are converting callers to real prospects—people who come in to see your house. Now it's a matter of dealing with strangers.

12

Showing Your House to Strangers

If you're going to sell FSBO, one thing you simply must get used to is showing your home to strangers. Literally hundreds of thousands of FSBO sellers do it all the time.

This is not to say that it is without risk. However, by being observant and cautious you can go a long way toward protecting yourself. And your first step usually begins with the prospect's phone call, which was discussed in Chapter 11.

Note: The following suggestions will not eliminate all risk to the FSBO seller. There is no way to do that short of not letting anyone into your home.

When a person calls about your home, in addition to their name and phone number, ask for their address. Often, if a person is willing to give an address, even if it happens to be an apartment or even a hotel room, it means that they are sincere about looking at your home for the purpose of purchasing. After all, how do they know you can't use a reverse phone book to check and see if their address is legitimate?

No, this system does not ensure that the caller is a prospective buyer and not a robber, but it helps. And it gives you the chance to call back and confirm your appointment before allowing anyone into your home.

How Should I Set Up Appointments?

When you've got your home for sale, you must make it available when a potential buyer wants to see it, not necessarily when it's convenient for you. If someone calls and wants to see it at four in the afternoon and you had planned on playing bridge at that time, cancel bridge and show the house. If a buyer calls at seven in the morning and wants to see the house at eight, if you're convinced he or she is a serious buyer, show it.

On the other hand, never show your home after dark. This is a simple safety precaution. It only stands to reason that if someone has harmful intentions, they will be more inclined to carry them out in the dark when it's harder to see what's going on.

In general, your home must be ready for showing almost anytime, and you must bend over backward to make time for buyers to see the place.

If you think this is a royal pain, you're right. It's inconvenient for you. It's imposing on you. It's downright frustrating. It's also necessary if you want to sell your home. A serious buyer is looking not only at your house but also at many other houses. If your home isn't available to see, that buyer will see another one and possibly buy it instead of yours.

By Appointment Only

My suggestion is that you hang a small sign onto your big FSBO sign (as well as attach a small note to your flyer) that says, "Shown By Appointment Only."

The reason here is it means potential buyers should call before coming by, which gives you a chance to get names, phone numbers, and addresses. It also gives you a chance to determine if prospects are legitimate and qualified. Of course, it also gives you a few moments to get your house cleaned up (it should, of course, already be in spotless condition!) before the prospect arrives.

Drop-Ins

No matter how much you indicate the house will be shown by appointment only, people will knock on the door and ask to see it right then. Be careful, but try not to turn them down.

Frequently, buyers cruise neighborhoods in which they are interested. They see your sign and think maybe your house is a possibility. Yes, it's shown by appointment only, but they don't have time to come back, or so they think. So they knock and ask if they can see it now. Chances are that they are serious buyers and you would risk losing a potential sale by not showing it.

On the other hand, drop-ins are totally unscreened. You don't know anything about them and you could be putting yourself at risk by letting them in. Below are my suggestions for showing the property. These five rules for screening drop-ins can't guarantee your safety, but they should help:

1. Before letting people in, get them to write down their names, addresses, and phone numbers. Serious buyers shouldn't hesitate to do this. At least confirm this in your phone book.

2. Ask questions such as those on the Phone Report (see Chapter 11).

3. Never let anyone into your house after dark. It's just too dangerous in the times in which we live. If it's a weekend in the afternoon and lots of people are around and about, you can consider it.

4. Never show the property when you are alone, particularly if you are a woman. Simply explain that it is an inconvenient time and offer to set up an appointment.

   Keep the drapes apart, the shutters and curtains open. This allows people from the outside to see in. No, it doesn't really offer any serious protection, but it may mean that someone with ill intent will think twice, knowing he or she may be seen.

Does doing all this mean a potential buyer will get away?

Yes, it could. But otherwise the risk is simply too great. Think of it this way: If your house were not up for sale, would you let in anyone who knocked on the door? The rules don't change that much when you're selling FSBO.

Showing the Home

Once you've determined that you have a potential buyer and not just another looker, the showing of the home is your next task. When you're setting up the appointment, try to leave yourself at least an hour, if possible. The reason is simple. You're going to have to do an awful lot of preparation before that potential buyer arrives at your FSBO. Figure 12.1 is a quick guide to getting your home ready to show.

How Can I Protect My Valuables?

Never, ever leave valuables in the home when you're showing. (That includes inside drawers.) Put them in a safety deposit box. Drop them off with friends or relatives.

The rule here is simple: If you don't leave something around that a person can walk off with, it won't get stolen. By the way, this applies whether you're selling FSBO or with an agent. (Agents can't watch buyers all the time, either.)

When the Potential Buyers Arrive

Greet all buyers warmly and ask friendly questions such as, "Did you have any trouble finding the house?" (if they called on an ad) or, "How did you happen to hear of our house?"

Another good starting point is to ask if the potential buyers have ever purchased a home from a FSBO. Chances are they haven't, so you can start up a conversation by pointing out that you're selling by owner to get a quick sale. You can note that one of the big benefits to a buyer of your not having to pay a full commission is a lower sales price. (Be sure that you do, in fact, have a lower sales price. See Chapter 9 for information on pricing.)

FIGURE 12.1
Checklist to Help You Prepare the House for Showing

1. Before the buyer arrives, be sure that your home is neat and clean. Things to be done include:
   - Vacuum carpets.
   - Sweep hallways.
   - Wash kitchen and bath floors.
   - Scrub sinks, toilets, tubs, and showers.
   - Wash and put away all dirty dishes.
   - Be sure countertops are clean, neat, and mostly empty.
   - Put away all loose clothing.
   - Make all beds.

2. Before the buyer arrives, be sure that you go around and turn on *all* the lights in the house. Even if it's the middle of the day, turn on all the lights. Buyers like homes that are light and airy, so having lots of lights on helps with this. Open all curtains and window shades as well.

3. Before the buyer arrives, check the odors in the house. Bathroom odors will offend most buyers. Use fresheners. Some clever sellers even have a pot boiling on the stove containing aromatic herbs or cookies baking in the oven, thus giving the house a warm, homey feel.

4. Before the buyer arrives, check the noise level. If there's no disturbing outside or inside noise, you're okay. If there are disturbing noises, such as someone working on the street, try turning on the stereo to a relaxing station. Be careful of playing rock and roll or other loud music. It may offend some buyers' tastes. (I don't suggest always turning on the stereo, as some agents do, because having low music on sometimes suggests to buyers that the scene has been artificially set. But if there's noise outside, then maybe even an artificially set scene is better.)

5. Before the buyer arrives, if it's in winter, light a fire in the fireplace so the house will feel warm and cozy. On an especially cold day, turn up the heat. In summer, be sure the air-conditioning (if you have it) is working and lower the temperature. You want the buyer to feel comfortable. (Note: An old trick that car salespeople use is to turn on the car's air-conditioning in a test drive. Marketing studies have shown that buyers are far more inclined to move positively when the temperature is just below 70 degrees!)

Once the buyers get into the house and you've established a rapport with them, think of the rule for showing:

RULE FOR SHOWING YOUR HOUSE

GET OUT OF THE BUYERS' WAY!

There's only one rule here, but it's important. It's like the old story about a thirsty horse: "You can lead a horse to water, but you can't make it drink."

The same applies to buyers. You can get them into your house, but you can't make them buy. The very worst thing you can do is point out every darling little nook and cranny, every precious thing that you have in your house.

Most buyers hate a pushy salesperson, and when that salesperson is the seller, they doubly hate it. The very best thing you can do, after welcoming them to your house and establishing rapport, is to get out of their way. Yes, you can walk around with them (to be sure they don't take anything), but it's best if you let them wander through your house and see it for themselves. (Remember, you should have removed valuables long before you let a prospect into your home. Remove them from inside drawers as well.)

Wise sellers often go out into the yard or the garage so that the buyers can be by themselves. Your goal is getting the buyers to feel comfortable in your home. They need to feel that they could live in your house and make it their own. They can't possibly do that if you stand next to them and keep pointing out ways that you've made the house your own.

There are two concerns here. The first, as we've already seen, is security. Leaving buyers alone in the house means that they can possibly take something of value while you're not there to notice. After all, even the most seemingly trustworthy buyers could still turn out to be crooks. You really don't know who these people are.

The second concern is that the buyers will overlook something important. For example, you may have oak wood floors, an important selling feature, but if the floors are covered with carpet, the buyers may not notice.

Yes, they may ask, but you should be ready to tell them in any case. You can address this situation in two ways. I suggest doing both. When the buyers first come in, hand them a sheet (which you've already prepared) describing all the best features of the house. (See Chapter 10 for what to include.) They can read the sheet as they walk through the house.

Second, when the potential buyers have had some time to walk through and look at the house (you can tell because they start coming out), it's a good idea to pop in and point out all the best features of your home. You may begin with a comment such as, "Did you notice that we have all hardwood oak floors under the carpet?" or "Did you see the fireplace in the master bedroom?"

You get the idea. You're simply giving the buyers information on features that they may have missed. Very often it will turn out that the buyers didn't really see all of the special features of your house and if they are interested, they may want to go back and look again. Accompany them this time and point out those features.

This is also a good time to begin a conversation about other concerns the potential buyers may have. You can talk about the proximity to schools and shopping. Buyers may want to know about the quality of the local schools as well as about the neighborhood and, in particular, your neighbors.

You can also talk about financing and any special terms you are offering. You may need to help the buyers understand how financing works.

In general, you want to be helpful. You want to give the buyers as much accurate information as possible.

One further point. Get time on your side. The longer the potential buyers hang around talking to you, the more they have invested in the house (in terms of time and commitment). If you can get potential buyers to stick around for an hour, you may get yourself a sale. On the other hand, don't give up on buyers just because they quickly walk through and leave. They may have another appointment. However, when you call back later, you may find out that they really did like your house. (We'll talk about the callback shortly.)

When Should I Try to Close?

Most of us would like to have the potential buyers walk through, ask a few questions, and then say, "We'll take it!"

It isn't likely to happen that way, at least not on this planet. Very few buyers will walk in, look at your house, and then agree to purchase. (The exception here is the buyers who have already looked at a lot of homes, have made up their minds on exactly what they want, and have determined quickly that your house fits their bill. It could happen, but you could grow old and gray waiting for such a deal to drop out of heaven.)

What's more likely to happen is that the buyers will spend some time looking at the house and talking with you, then leave. Perhaps a few days later, they will call (or you'll call them) and want to see it again. Buyers may need to see the house several times before actually deciding that they want to buy. That's far more likely to be the scenario.

Therefore, it's important that you don't try to close on the first showing. The seller who lets the buyers walk through and then says, "Okay, let's draw up the deal," appears naïve, puts the buyers on the spot, and could lose the sale. Don't appear to be pressuring the buyers. Doing so would only backfire.

Wait until the buyers call back or until you call them. Then you can ask a few questions to determine if they are really interested.

Should I Hold an Open House?

Real estate agents are always holding open houses. They seem to be a backbone of home sales. If it works for agents, will it work for you? As a FSBO seller should you hold your own open house?

No, probably not.

First, let's understand what an agent hopes to accomplish with an open house. Numerous studies have clearly shown that almost never does a buyer who comes to an open house actually buy that particular house.

This does not mean that open houses attract only lookers. Quite the contrary, they attract sincere buyers. It's just that they are most frequently not buyers for the house that's open.

Agents hold open houses mainly to find potential clients. Yes, they show the house that's open, but when a buyer doesn't fit, they try to work with that buyer to find a house he or she does want. In other words, for agents open houses are a major source of picking up clients, both buyers and sometimes sellers who have to get rid of their existing house before they can purchase.

You, on the other hand, have only one house to sell. If the people coming through don't want to purchase your home, you can't very well interest them in another property or offer to list their existing homes. Thus, in theory, if the vast majority of people who stop won't want to purchase your house, holding an open house is largely a waste of your time.

I said in theory. In practice, remember that your house is open virtually all the time. Anytime buyers want to see it, all they have to do is call up, give a name, phone number, and address, and you'll show it to them.

Show It to Your Neighbors

On the other hand, it's a good idea to hold at least one open house so that your neighbors have a chance to come by and look at your home. The reason simply is that one of your neighbors may want to buy your home, or have a relative or friend who does, or may be able to suggest someone else who is looking for a place just like yours.

Neighbors can be an important source of prospects. Therefore, I suggest you try at least one open house on a Sunday. Don't advertise it. Just stick an "Open House" sign in your front yard (readily available in most drug stores).

Mostly you'll get your neighbors. Take the usual security precautions of having several people home, in the daytime, with any valuables locked up. Then welcome everyone (though not necessarily including the neighborhood kids, dogs, and cats).

Should I Call Back the Prospect?

Perhaps the most important call you'll make when selling your property is the callback. Some buyers came out, gave you their names, addresses, and phone numbers, looked at your house, and left. If you don't call them back, you may never see them again. Also, you may lose a deal that could have been made.

I can't think of the number of times I've called back potential buyers only to have them tell me, "Yes, we were thinking about your house. It's really nice, we like it, and probably would make an offer on it. But we just never got around to calling you."

Don't wait for buyers to call you. Almost all buyers suffer from a kind of forgetfulness that sets in as soon as they see your property. I suspect that it comes about because they feel if they call you back, you'll think that they surely want it, will pay full price, will give you cash, and will meet all your other terms. They may simply be afraid to call you for fear of giving you the wrong impression. (Translate that to mean a strong bargaining position.)

I can recall talking to buyers who were actually mad at agents (in this case) who didn't call them back when they were really interested in the house. "That so-and-so agent dropped me. What kind of irresponsible action is that?"

I sometimes remind such people that a phone line works both ways: If they were really interested, they could call the agent or the seller direct, but, somehow, they just never do.

The point is, don't wait around for potential buyers to call you. After a day or two, call back. It could make you a deal.

What Should I Say on the Callback?

Obviously you will introduce yourself, mention the house they saw, and then ask something like, "Did you have any further thoughts on the house?" or "Was there something more about the house you'd like to see?" (thereby offering to show it again).

If the potential buyer reacts by saying, yes, he or she really did like the house and would like to see it again or, miracle of miracles, "Yes, I'd like to talk about a deal with you," you're on your way.

More than likely, however, the buyer will be restrained, non-committal, and try to get off the phone as quickly as possible. If that's the case, you probably have a looker and not a buyer (at least not for your house). However, don't give up. Just because you don't get a yes right off the bat doesn't mean that you're getting a no.

Always Ask, "What's Wrong?"

After a bit of small talk, ask what's wrong with your house. This is not to say that there is anything wrong with the place. What you should try to determine, however, is what the buyers see as a problem. In other words, find out the buyers' main objection to your property. You might ask a question such as "What about the property doesn't appeal to you?" or "Is there something about the house that you don't like?"

The potential buyers, if they are even remotely interested in the property, should now explain to you why they aren't willing to buy it. The reasons they give could be anything, but Figure 12.2 gives a few of the more common ones.

If you can get a single, good reason why they don't want to buy the house, chances are that you've got real buyers on your hands. Now, all you have to do is turn that negative into a positive and you've got a sale.

FIGURE 12.2
Common Reasons Given for Not Buying

1. Not the right location

2. Too big/small, not enough/too many bedrooms

3. Too expensive/poor terms

4. Poor condition

5. Lacks features (air-conditioning, central heating, new carpeting, big yard, etc.)

Turning a Negative into a Positive

Usually you can turn a negative into a positive. For example, if the problem is price or terms, you can agree to negotiate. This should heat up the buyers' enthusiasm and should result in both of you getting together to discuss things further.

On the other hand, if the house is in the wrong location, there's very little you can say or do. You can point out, for example, "For the location, the price is very good. If you want a better location, you're going to have to pay a whole lot more. Do you have that much more money to spend?"

If the buyers don't have enough money to move to a better location, then you're dealing with the champagne taste and beer pocketbook mentality. Your job is to convince the buyers of the reality of the real estate market. Ask them if they've looked around at other houses. (You should have already done this yourself when you established the price.) Explain to them that for what they want to spend, they simply won't be able to do better than your house. In short, try to bring them down to reality.

On the other hand, if it turns out that they can spend more money for a better area, you can point out that they can also spend less. Why spend more when they can have all the features of your house for less money?

FIGURE 12.3
How to Deal with Buyers' Objections

1. Turn a negative into a positive.

2. Try to get them to come and see the house again.

3. Don't give up.

You won't overcome every potential buyer's objections with this strategy, but it's worth a shot. Be creative. As long as you're on the phone, you've still got a potential deal. My suggestion is that no matter how negative the answers may seem, try to follow the rules for dealing with potential buyers' objections given in Figure 12.3.

If the buyers simply aren't interested, don't want to talk anymore, and say "Good-bye!" well, it's just one that got away, for today. My suggestion is to put their names on a back page and call again in two or three weeks. Maybe they will have seen more of the market and rethought their priorities.

Yes, you may make a bit of a pest out of yourself. But if you're polite, charming, and even, if possible, witty, they'll overlook that. After all, many sales are made simply because the seller is persistent.

Create a Visitor Book

Ask everyone who comes to see your house to sign a visitor book if he or she might even remotely be perceived as a serious buyer. If you ask visitors to do this just as they come into the house, most people will be happy to oblige as a courtesy to you.

The visitor book should provide space for the minimal information: name, address, and phone number. You can also solicit written comments. Some sellers ask visitors to indicate the kind of property they are looking for (number of bedrooms and bathrooms, location, price, etc.) as a way of determining who is a more likely buyer than another.

There are two purposes for having visitors sign the book. The first is to provide you with a means of contacting them later on. (See the previous phone callback discussion.)

The second is to provide the name and address of every buyer who came by in the event that you later list the property. You can specify in the listing, even in an exclusive-right-to-sell listing, that if anyone to whom you showed the house before the listing term buys it, you don't have to pay a commission. Your visitor book is the proof of who was there and who wasn't.

Don't underestimate the value of the visitor book. It can lead you back to a looker who becomes a buyer. It can save you a commission. A FSBO seller who doesn't have a visitor book is overlooking an enormous resource.

Note: Any book or even a sheet of paper will do. However, if you go to the stationery store, you can pick up ready-made visitor books. Usually they are designed for receptions or weddings, but they can easily fill the need here. Just be sure that at the top of each page, you clearly print (or type) the information you want visitors to record. See Figure 12.4 for an example of a visitor's book and the type of information you want to record.

When You Get a Real Live Buyer

One of these days, perhaps sooner than you imagined, you will find a buyer who says, "Yes, I want to purchase your home." You will haggle over the price, the terms, and perhaps even the light fixture in the dining room, but ultimately, the buyer will want to purchase and you'll sag back with a sigh of relief telling yourself, "At last, it's over!"

FIGURE 12.4
Typical Visitor Book

Our Address: 2341 Maple St.
Our Phone: 555-4352

Thanks for looking at our For Sale By Owner home. So that we have a record of those people who stop by, please list the following information:

Name _____

Phone Number _____

Address _____

City, State, ZIP _____

Comments _____

Name _____

Phone Number _____

Address _____

City, State, ZIP _____

Comments _____

Name _____

Phone Number _____

Address _____

City, State, ZIP _____

Comments _____

Name _____

Phone Number _____

Address _____

City, State, ZIP _____

Comments _____

Step-by-Step to Writing a Sales Agreement

CAUTION

Do not attempt to complete a sales agreement bought at a stationery store or taken out of any book until you've read this chapter!

Many would-be FSBO sellers ask themselves questions such as, "If I do find a buyer, what do I use to get him or her to sign up? What document do I use for the purchase? Do I accept a check as a deposit and, if so, should I give a receipt? What should that receipt say?"

The devil is in the paperwork. You may be excellent at finding a buyer, but then, suddenly, you can run out of steam. How do you handle the machinations of the actual written transaction?

Is the Paperwork Really That Difficult?

Can't anyone fill out a sales agreement and a receipt for a deposit? After all, how hard can it be?

The honest answer is that it is both simple and complex. Yes, you can do it yourself, but you'd be wise leaving it to an expert. The legalities behind the paperwork can get you into trouble later on down the road, if you don't know what you're doing.

What Is the Sales Agreement/Deposit Receipt?

It's the backbone of the sale. The paper that documents a sale in real estate is called, naturally enough, the sales agreement (also known as the purchase agreement). It should include all the terms and conditions of the sale.

To understand how a sales agreement is put together today, however, a short jaunt into the past is helpful. When I started in real estate more than 30 years ago in California, we didn't use a sales agreement. Instead, we used a deposit receipt. The deposit receipt, in fact, is still used in many areas.

A deposit receipt is just what it says it is. It's a receipt for a deposit on a piece of property that the buyer gives to the agent or the seller. (Until the buyer puts up some earnest money or a deposit, you really don't have a solid deal.) As part of the receipt, however, all the terms and conditions of the sale were specified. Hence, it became, in effect, a sales agreement.

Back then, the deposit receipt used to be one legal page long. At the top it contained space to fill in such obvious information as the correct address of the property, the name of the buyer, and the amount of the offer (purchase price).

Then a paragraph of legalese specified that the buyer was going to purchase the property according to the terms following, that "time was of the essence" (meaning the deal had to close by a certain date), and a few other conditions. About two-thirds of the remaining page consisted of blank lines. Someone—the seller, the buyer, or the agent—filled in all the terms.

Finally, there were places for all parties to sign and date the document at the bottom.

Keep in mind that the legal language on this simple document was only a few paragraphs. The agent, the seller, or the buyer filled in everything else by hand.

This old deposit receipt form served its function well. It was used to facilitate the sale of millions of pieces of property for decades. However, it had a serious flaw—in many cases, it wasn't legally binding.

A seller or a buyer who wanted to get out of the transaction for any reason without penalty frequently could go to court and demonstrate that the document didn't really represent what was intended. Either party could say that the agreement's language was vague or inaccurate or misrepresented their intentions.

Because the deposit receipt was mostly handwritten by agents, sellers, or buyers, not by lawyers familiar with creating legally binding language, these contentions were often correct. In other words, the deposit receipt often was fatally flawed. It was rarely the legally binding document intended.

This placed a burden on agents. If either a buyer or a seller got out of a deal because of a flawed deposit receipt written by an agent, the party who felt injured often sued the agent. As a result, such lawsuits increased in the 1970s and agents became gun-shy. When coupled with the skyrocketing price of real estate at the end of the 1970s, the litigation began to involve serious money.

Band-Aids

To correct the situation, agents had their attorneys create sales agreements where more of the language was formally printed. Many of the paragraphs that the agents used to write in were now created by lawyers and included as part of the agreement. Instead of a single page of mostly blank lines, these new sales agreements were often two pages long with mostly printed text and only a few paragraphs where the agents would write in the terms of the sale.

The problem, of course, was that any time the agent, or the seller or buyer, wrote in anything at all, there was a chance it wouldn't be legally binding because of incorrect language used. By the late 1980s, litigation had demonstrated that even these new contracts with a minimum of language inserted by the agent, buyer, or seller could prove to be a minefield. An innocuous sentence inserted by a seller at the time the sales agreement was signed could provide a way out for a buyer later on. The seller might tie up the house for months only to discover that the buyer could walk away from the deal and be entitled to a full return of the deposit! Or worse, even after the sale was consummated, the seller had moved out, and the buyer moved in, inexact language in the contract and an angry buyer might result in litigation in which the seller was forced to pay damages to the buyer.

Today's Sales Agreement

This brings us to the present. Today the consensus seems to be that if it isn't written in by a lawyer, it isn't accurate or binding. Hence, we have the extraordinary situation in which agents are using sales agreements that are often seven, eight, ten, or more pages in length. The entire document is a preprinted form and paragraphs for various contingencies are listed. All that the agent, buyer, or seller need do is write in the correct names of the parties involved and the property description, check and initial the appropriate paragraphs, and fill in the sales price and loan amount. No other writing on the document is recommended.

Furthermore, while state real estate groups usually prepare these forms for their agents/members to use, large real estate franchise companies such as Coldwell Banker or CENTURY 21® have their attorneys prepare their own forms. Thus, there may be dozens of different formally prepared sales agreements that are used for real estate transactions, even within a given city.

The Plight of the FSBO

Needless to say, this puts a FSBO seller at a disadvantage. You don't have your property listed and, as a consequence, you don't have an agent's sales agreement. Yet, to lock up a buyer, you do need a sales agreement that records a receipt for a deposit and spells out the terms of the sale. What do you do?

One answer used by some FSBO sellers, unwisely in my opinion, is to finesse the whole problem by simply going to their local stationery store and purchasing a form called something like "Sales Agreement for Real Property." A variety of these are put out by several publishing companies, and they contain all of the basics; although in truth, they often tend to contain more blank space than legal language. Use of these forms may be asking for trouble.

Other FSBO sellers may have a friend who is an agent, from whom they ask to borrow a couple of sales agreement forms. Because most agents are eager to cooperate with FSBOs in any way, hoping that if the property doesn't sell they will eventually get a listing, they cooperate and hand over some of the forms. (Most agents, however, will first scrupulously cross the name of their company off the form, hoping to avoid any legal entanglements later on.)

Where does this leave the FSBO seller? In a sense, it leaves you not much better off than you were before. You have a form to use, but unless you're an attorney or very experienced in selling your own real estate (in which case you probably don't need this kit), you still don't possess the knowledge to fill in the form correctly, even down to knowing which boxes to check and which to leave blank.

The fact remains that if you accept a buyer's deposit, write in the terms of the sale on the document, and do the job badly, you could be laying the groundwork for a lot of expensive litigation later on.

The Wrong Way, the Easy Way, the Right Way

This discussion is not intended to frighten you away from handling a FSBO sale because of the paperwork. It's intended only to present a background for some of the problems. There are, however, solutions—good ones.

Here's one that could work well for you. If you are relatively new to selling property on your own, then don't attempt to handle the sales agreement at all. Instead, have someone else who is knowledgeable do it for you.

Using an agent first comes to mind. Because we've already covered the use of a fee-for-service agent and a discount broker for these purposes in Chapters 4 and 5, it might be a good idea at this juncture to explain how to use an attorney for these services.

When to Use a Real Estate Attorney

In many states, attorneys who specialize in real estate abound. They make a living by handling the formalities of real estate transactions. Often they prepare the documents necessary to complete a deal.

Why not contact one of these attorneys before you find a buyer and work out an arrangement? The arrangement will go something like this: You will bring in a buyer who has agreed to purchase your home according to certain negotiated terms; the two of you will sit down and the attorney will draw up the sales agreement; the buyer will then examine the document (and perhaps have his or her own attorney examine it); and then you will both sign it.

Simple? Easy? Quick? And it relieves you of the burden of having to worry about correctly filling out a sales agreement, something you probably can't do.

But what about the cost? Keep in mind that we're talking about an attorney who specializes in real estate transactions. Often these lawyers get as little as $500 to $1,500 for doing the documentary work related to a sale. Just be sure that you make an arrangement with the attorney before you need legal services. Your attorney will let you know what information you will need to supply beforehand, so that when you come in, you will have all of it ready.

Dealing with a Nervous Buyer

A big advantage of using either a fee-for-service agent, a discount broker, or an attorney when you're a FSBO seller is dealing with a nervous buyer. One of the problems with selling FSBO is that buyers tend to be nervous. They tend to be wary of signing anything. Thus, even after you have a buyer who is ready, willing, and able to purchase your home, he or she may not want to commit directly to you. After all, the buyer may think, "How am I protected from an unscrupulous seller who wants to cheat me?"

Further, it is a rare buyer who is willing to give a deposit check directly to the seller. As buyers ought to know, once the seller receives that deposit check, it's his or her money. True, as a seller, you might have to pay it back sometime in the future if the deal goes sour. However, until that time, you can stick the money in your account and spend it. If I were a buyer, the last thing in the world I would want to do would be to give my deposit directly to the seller.

However, the real estate agent or attorney provides a reasonable third party for the buyer. A document prepared by the seller may have questionable validity. Buyers are likely to have greater confidence when the agreement is drawn up by an agent or attorney. Furthermore, the buyer can question the agent or attorney and, presumably, get accurate answers.

Also, the buyer can turn the deposit over to the agent or the attorney, who may then turn it over to an escrow company after the sales agreement is filled out and signed. In short, the attorney or agent becomes a great facilitator for you.

Don'ts

We've already suggested one area that might be a minefield for you: filling out the sales agreement yourself without proper knowledge. Another is having someone who isn't really qualified do it, such as an escrow officer (or even an unqualified agent).

In the past, escrow officers were often obliging to sellers and buyers and would help them create a sales agreement. However, the purpose of escrow is to act as an independent third party in fulfilling the instructions of the deposit receipt. While escrow officers are normally well versed in following instructions, they may be less than adequate in creating them.

As a result, some escrow officers have painfully found themselves at the center of disputes that came about from sales agreements they helped to create. Thus, to protect themselves, today few escrow officers will help you with your sales agreement. Rather, after you have the agreement filled out and signed, they will simply aid you in seeing that its conditions are carried out.

Finally, be careful of friends who are supposedly knowledgeable in real estate and who offer to lend a helping hand. Your friend may, indeed, have successfully bought and sold a half-dozen properties, but he or she may simply not have the very specific information needed for your particular transaction. That ignorance could get you in trouble.

Doing It Yourself

Okay, you've been warned about the problems. Now, how do you get it done right?

The following six steps, to be taken in order, provide the FSBO seller a step-by-step guide to obtaining a solid sales agreement:

1. *Find a buyer.* Here we're making the assumption that you already have the buyer and need to move forward with the paperwork.

2. *Agree on the terms.* Having a buyer is one thing. Having a buyer who's ready, willing, and able to purchase at the price and terms for which you're willing to sell is quite something else. Probably the next most important thing after finding a buyer is coming to an agreement on price and terms.

3. *Fill out a worksheet.* At this point, many agents use a worksheet that includes the areas that are negotiable. By going down the worksheet and filling in the blanks, you can quickly see if you and the buyer agree on the important points as well as those you must negotiate.

4. *Take the worksheet to your agent or attorney.* From the worksheet, your agent or attorney should help you prepare a formal sales agreement.

5. *Sign the agreement.* Have the buyer sign the agreement and give you a check made payable to the attorney's escrow account or a licensed escrow company.

6. *Take the check and the agreement to escrow.* Open an escrow account. You've just passed the biggest document hurdle!

Filling Out a Sales Worksheet

Figure 13.1 is a worksheet that I have found to be particularly useful. Keep in mind that this is a worksheet here, not the sales agreement. The purpose of this worksheet is to set down in writing all of the things that you and the buyer agree on.

FACT

Getting the terms in writing is important. Often when two people speak, particularly two who may be in an adversarial relationship such as buyer and seller, they misunderstand each other. You may say something that the buyer misinterprets as a concession and vice versa. The whole point of preparing the worksheet is that you and the buyer can sit down together and put in writing exactly what the terms of the sale are.

Nobody signs the worksheet. Once you've filled in the terms, you and the buyer can take the worksheet to an attorney or agent who can correctly fill out a sales agreement that you can sign.

Furthermore, because neither you nor the buyer is actually going to sign this worksheet and because by itself it's not any sort of a binding agreement, it is extremely useful as a negotiating tool. There may be some point of disagreement between you and the buyer—perhaps the matter of the down payment or the interest rate on a loan you are carrying back. You can reasonably say to the buyer, "Let's sit down and see if we can work it out on paper. This is just a worksheet. I'm not going to sign it and neither are you. We'll just put the numbers down and see if we can work it out."

The worksheet now becomes a tool for trying out different ideas and numbers. Using the worksheet, you may be able to make a deal with a buyer that you might otherwise lose.

Be Sure You Understand the Sales Agreement Worksheet

Because the worksheet is the most important tool you have when it comes time to hammer out the sales price and terms, you should be clear on what it should contain. Let's take it one step at a time:

☑ **FIGURE 13.1**
FSBO Sales Worksheet

Address of property_____

Buyer's name _____

Seller's name _____

Price $_____

Deposit $_____

Cash down $_____

(In addition to deposit)

First mortgage $_____

      Assume _____? New _____?

      Interest rate _____%

      Fixed _____? Adj. _____?

      Term _____? Pts. _____?

Second mortgage $_____

      Assume _____? New _____?

      Interest rate _____%

      Fixed _____? Adj. _____?

      Term _____? Pts. _____?

Third mortgage $_____

      Assume _____? New _____?

      Interest rate _____%

      Fixed _____? Adj. _____?

      Term _____? Pts. _____?

Total $ _____

(Must equal price)

Other conditions of sale

_____

_____

The date the escrow will close _____

The date the buyer will get occupancy _____

The real estate attorney to be used _____

The escrow company to be used _____

Sales price. Most people start here and it is a good idea to at least get an offering price down. However, often the sales price comes about as the result of a combination of how much money the buyer can put down and how big a mortgage he or she can negotiate. Put down an offering price, but be sure it's in pencil so that you can scratch it out as negotiations continue.

Deposit. Sellers usually want a big deposit because they know that the bigger the deposit, the bigger the buyer's commitment to the deal. Buyers, on the other hand, often want a lower deposit because it means they are tying up less money.

There is no rule on how big the deposit should be. It should be large enough, however, to convince you that the buyer is serious. Many agents have a hard-and-fast rule that the deposit should be $5,000, regardless of the purchase price. That hardly makes sense on lower-priced properties and may be insufficient on higher-priced ones. Here's a schedule of how big a deposit I usually want from a buyer when I am selling a house:

Deposit Schedule

To $50,000	$1,000 minimum up to 5%
$50,000 to $100,000	$2,000 minimum up to 3%
$100,000 to $300,000	$3,000 minimum up to 3%
Over $300,000	$5,000 minimum up to 3%

Keep in mind that the deposit is what money you may be entitled to receive if the buyer can't complete the transaction. If the sales agreement is properly drawn and the buyer doesn't perform as promised through no fault of your own, you may get the money. In most cases, however, extenuating circumstances allow the buyer to back out of the deal and get his or her money back. Don't make the mistake of aiming for the deposit. Your goal is not to get the deposit, it is to sell your house.

Mortgages. This is the trickiest area for most people. If you're like most FSBO sellers, you know something, but not a great deal, about financing a real estate purchase. Thus, you may feel inadequate dealing with the issue of mortgages.

However, because virtually all real estate transactions are financed (almost no one pays cash these days), you'll have to know at least enough to get by.

We'll cover what you need to know in Chapter 14. For now, let's say that you can help the buyer by at least jotting down the amount of the mortgage(s), the estimated interest rate, points, term, and type (fixed or adjustable rate).

Note: It is important that when you jot down items such as interest rate and points (points, by the way, represent percentage points of the mortgage amount—three points on a $100,000 mortgage is equal to $3,000) list them at a higher level than you can reasonably expect to get at the current time. The reason is that these rates fluctuate. You don't want to lose a buyer because interest rates jumped up half a percent or points jumped between the time you hammered out the agreement and the sale was ready to close.

Terms. This, of course, is the toughest area of all. As noted earlier, this is the area where agents got into trouble in the past. If you don't try to add a bunch of legalese, however, and leave the actual writing of the terms to your attorney, you shouldn't have much of a hassle in this area.

Terms may include such items as the following:

- *How long does the buyer have to qualify for the mortgage?* You don't want to take your property off the market unless you're sure the buyer will qualify. Typically, the buyer may be entitled to a full refund of the deposit if he or she can't get the mortgage. You may want to specify that the buyer has a week to get preliminary loan approval or four weeks for final loan approval.
- *What personal property will be included in the sale?* Typically, buyers want all flooring, window coverings, and fixtures. You may want to specify that a favorite ceiling lamp in the dining room, for example, is not included in the sale.

- *Are there any conditions that must be met before the sale can be completed?* Buyers may want "subject to" or contingency clauses included. For example, they may insist that the sale be subject to their recreational vehicle fitting along the side of the house. You may allow them a day or two to take measurements to be sure. On the other hand, they may insist on the sale being contingent upon the sale of their current home. You may not want to tie up your property waiting for them to sell theirs, or you may insist that, yes, you'll give them right of first refusal on a sale provided that you can keep your house on the market. The term *right of first refusal* usually means that in the event you find a cash buyer before the buyers who made the first offer sell their current home, they have a set time, typically 72 hours, to remove the contingency or lose the deal.

- *What inspections, if any, are you going to have?* In the past, there used to be one basic inspection—for termites and fungus infestation. The reason for this inspection was that most lenders required a clearance before they would fund a mortgage. In recent years, however, many things have changed, not the least of which are inspections. Today, it's a wise seller who insists that the buyer have the home inspected by a competent building inspector (and some states require it). We'll have much more to say about home inspections in Chapter 16.

NOTE

Insisting that the buyer have inspections is also a selling feature. If you, the FSBO seller, agree to an inspection, most buyers will feel that you're not holding anything back.

- *State any other terms.* Everything in real estate is negotiable. Your buyer may wish to insert some strange condition that you've never heard of. If you agree to it, put it down in writing. Anything can be included. However, your real estate attorney should advise you about the wisdom of the particular terms you and the buyer want inserted.

And so forth. The terms can consist of almost anything. Your goal here is not to write them in legalese, but to get them down as clearly and succinctly as possible so that both you and the buyer know what the terms are and agree on them. Let the agent or attorney handle the written details.

A helpful hint is to have as few terms as possible and make those few as short as possible. The more terms you have, the greater your chance of losing the deal through a misunderstanding or disagreement.

Include dates. All real estate transactions are based on performance over time. As the seller, you should be willing to give the buyer a reasonable amount of time to arrange a loan. However, you don't want the transaction to drag on interminably. Typically, financing can be arranged within 45 days. Therefore, you will want to agree with the buyer on a date for the close of escrow and the time when the title will transfer and you'll get your sale and money.

Keep in mind that while you will agree to this date, it will be arbitrary. Things can happen that can cause delays, including financing problems on the buyer's part or, perhaps, difficulties in clearing title on your part. However, the date is what you will be aiming at. Your attorney will want to add language explaining what will happen to the deposit in the event the sale doesn't close by the appointed date or if it doesn't close at all. (See the previous section on deposits.)

The date of occupancy or when the buyer takes possession of the property is often the same date as the close of escrow, but it doesn't have to be. It can be any date you and the buyer agree on. However, in most cases you would be wise not to let the buyer occupy the property until the deal has closed and title has transferred. The reason, simply, is that if the buyer takes possession of the property and then, for any reason, can't close the deal, you not only haven't sold your house, but you've got someone in it who you now may have to go to court to evict!

Include names. It's a good idea to name the real estate agent or attorney, the title insurance company, and the escrow company that you will use in the transaction. Because the buyer will be filling out this form with you, you will quickly discover if he or she has any preferences. If so, you may wish to accede to them, particularly in the case of escrow and title companies. (While their fees differ slightly, most are close in price and perform similar services.)

NOTE

The Real Estate Settlement Procedures Act (RESPA) may prohibit you as a seller from insisting on a particular title insurance or escrow company.

You will, however, probably want to insist on the real estate attorney or agent who has already agreed to write up the deal. If the buyer insists on using his or her own attorney or agent, then you may want to arrange a meeting at which both will be present, your attorney/agent and the buyer's.

In this chapter, we've looked at the most important piece of documentation you will have as part of the transaction, the sales agreement/deposit receipt. Getting this document done right helps ensure a successful transaction.

14

Financing the Sale

How do you respond when a buyer seems interested in your home and then asks, "What kind of a mortgage can I get on this place?"

Sure, it would be nice if a buyer came in and offered to pay for your home in cash, but don't expect it to happen any time soon. Almost all residential real estate is financed–your buyer will need a mortgage. The trouble is that many buyers are financing-illiterate. They don't know a thing about getting a loan. So if you want a sale, it's up to you to help them.

There's really nothing new or different about this. If an agent were involved, that person would help the buyer get to the financing. The agent would determine if that person could afford your home. But when selling FSBO, the agent's not here to do it, so it's up to you.

How Do I Know If the Buyer Can Afford My House?

A good rule of thumb is that many people who look at your house can't really afford to buy it. Of course, the lower your home is priced and the higher the typical income in your area, the more people will be able to afford it. The higher your price and the lower the typical income, the fewer.

What this means is that when you eventually get someone who says he or she is ready and willing to purchase, your first move must be to determine *if* he or she really can do so. It may turn out that the thrill of getting a buyer will rapidly fade when you discover that the buyer has bad credit, doesn't have enough income, or doesn't have a large enough bank account to make the purchase.

Of course, it's up to a lender (assuming you're not offering seller financing) to actually make the determination. However, it won't hurt you to at least get an idea if the buyer's in the ballpark.

How Do I Broach Credit Worthiness and Income with a Buyer?

Because you are the seller, many buyers will hesitate to reveal necessary financial information to you. They may fear that you will use it to gain leverage in negotiating the price. Or they may simply feel that it's none of your business.

On the other hand, you need to know some basic information. Can the buyers get a large enough loan to afford your home?

The real trick is to get the information without scaring away the buyers. My suggestion is that you do *not* simply come out and ask such direct questions as, "How large a loan can you get?" or "Do you have any bad credit?" The buyers may simply decide that you're too nosy and may take their business elsewhere.

On the other hand, I suggest that you *do* drop hints early on about what it takes to buy your home. For example, as the buyers begin to show significant interest, you can explain that if they plan to put down 20 percent, their payments at then-current interest rates will likely be around $X per month. If they put down 10 percent, the monthly payment increases to $X a month. At 5 percent down, it's even more. All plus taxes and insurance.

You can watch their reactions. Do they seem to feel that's acceptable? Or do they blink, look astonished, and give the impression that it's an impossibly high figure? If it's the latter, I wouldn't start sending out change of address notices quite yet.

Once the buyers are very interested and are ready to make an offer, I suggest you first ask them if they are "preapproved?" If so, ask to see the preapproval letter. It should contain if not the maximum amount the buyer can get in a mortgage, then at least the maximum monthly payment. And from that, any amortization table can quickly get you to the maximum price, given the current interest rates. (Amortization tables are widely available online at most mortgage lending Web sites, which we'll discuss later in this chapter.)

Has the Buyer Been Preapproved?

Preapproval is exceedingly common in today's marketplace. The buyer goes to a lender, usually a mortgage broker, and the broker helps him or her fill out a standard mortgage application.

F A C T

A mortgage broker is a company or an individual who brokers mortgages. The broker does not lend his or her own money, but arranges financing from banks and other lending institutions. In today's marketplace, mortgage brokers probably account for a majority of all residential real estate financing.

Next the broker submits the form to a lender, who runs a credit check, and finally, if done correctly, runs the whole thing by the underwriters. With today's technology, it can quickly be determined how much of a monthly payment the buyer can afford and how big a mortgage that translates into. This is put into a letter that the buyer can give to you.

If the negotiations get serious, it's not unreasonable to ask to see such a preapproval letter. If the buyers are serious and they have one, they'll show it to you.

If they haven't got one, then you should suggest they get it. You can point out that they'll need it no matter what home they try to buy, yours or someone else's. And, hopefully, you've done your homework so you can send them to a mortgage broker who can quickly check their income and credit and get such a letter out. (Today, you can get preapproved in a day or two.)

Don't Get Pushy

Beyond following the suggestions offered above, I caution that you not go any further in qualifying your buyers. If they have a legitimate preapproval letter for enough to buy your home, it's not exactly like money in the bank, but it's close. Get started on the Sales Agreement Worksheet in Chapter 13 and reach a consensus on terms and price. Take it to your agent or attorney and you're on your way to a sale. (Be sure the agreement specifies a time limit for the buyers to get approval for funding of their mortgage.)

On the other hand, you may be asked by the buyers at any stage along the way about the kind of seller financing, if any, that's available on the property. Again, you should have done your homework and be ready to give the appropriate answers. We'll discuss this in greater detail later in this chapter.

What If the Buyers Aren't Preapproved?

If the buyers aren't preapproved, then it's in your best interest to ask them to go through the process. But perhaps you want to tie them into the purchase before then. If they say they're sure they can get a mortgage, it's not unreasonable to request a clause in the sales agreement that asks them to prove it. This clause would typically say that the buyers will be preapproved by a lender within a reasonably short amount of time, say a week or two. If they don't get such firm preapproval (defined shortly), then the deal is null and void.

Remember, if the buyers can't get financing and you go forward with the sale, you'll be taking your house off the market and tying it up perhaps for months before finding out they really can't buy.

If the buyers protest the clause, I suggest that you explain the problem to them in exactly those terms. They now want to buy and are probably eager to do so. You've agreed on a price. However, before you agree to take your house off the market for an extended period of time, you need to know that they can get necessary financing. It's not a bit unreasonable.

A Lender's Firm Commitment Is Better

While preapproval letters are indeed nice, they are not a guarantee. Most of them say the same thing, namely that if the buyers' credit doesn't change, and if they have the money in the bank that they claim, then they probably can get a loan.

What you would ideally like is a firm commitment by a lender. This is a bit different. It says that the lender (not the mortgage broker, but the company actually lending the mortgage money) has checked out the buyers—has checked not only their credit, but verified their income/employment and their money on deposit—and says that they will definitely offer those buyers a mortgage.

A preapproval letter is a good start. But you can take a firm commitment to the bank. (Usually, extenuating circumstances such as a job loss or illness also can quash a supposed "sure thing" mortgage.)

Can't I Just Approve the Buyers Myself?

Not if they're getting an institutional loan (in other words, a loan not from you). Today, getting "approved" means getting a detailed financial background sheet, doing a credit report, getting a good credit score on FICO (Fair, Issac and Company) as well as having sufficient money to make the down payment. Buyers just aren't going to want to give you that kind of information. And, quite frankly, it's none of the seller's business. You really only want to be assured that the buyers can get a loan, not become their financial advisor.

Suffice to say that there are all sorts of things that can derail an otherwise ready-to-go buyer. Past bankruptcies, foreclosures, delinquent or missed payments—all can shoot a buyer down. And these should be reflected in the preapproval letter (or lack of it) that your buyer obtains.

What If I'm Offering Seller Financing?

This a different story. If you're offering seller financing—usually a second mortgage—as part of the purchase price, then you have every right to personally approve the buyers' credit. Here's how in the following figure.

Have the buyers fill out a qualification sheet. You can use the chart in Figure 14.1 to qualify buyers who are asking you for seller financing. It asks only for a minimum of information, yet will at least give you a good idea of whether your buyer is likely to be able to pay back your loan.

How to Use the Buyer Qualification Chart

If the buyers fill out the buyer qualification chart even partially, you may get enough information to determine quickly if they qualify for the loan they are requesting on your property. Keep in mind, however, that you can only request this information—you can't demand it. If the buyers refuse, then you may simply not want to give them seller financing.

Monthly Gross Income

Most buyers won't hesitate to tell you their monthly gross income. They usually understand that income is critical to buying a property, and they will want to let you know that they make enough to qualify.

What you need to know is that all of their mortgage payments, including the first they'll get from the lender as well as the second from you plus taxes and insurance, should not equal more than around a third of their gross income. Lender's studies indicate that often if the total house payments are higher, there's a better chance the borrower won't be able to make the payments and you'll have to.

If your buyers indicate sufficient income, don't rejoice quite yet. Keep in mind that from their total income, lenders subtract any long-term payments (typically those lasting four months or

FIGURE 14.1
Buyer Qualification Chart

Name _____

Address _____

Phone Number _____

Income _____

What is your monthly gross income?

    Husband $_____

    Wife $_____

    Other source $_____

    Total $_____

What are the monthly payments on your long-term debt including:

    Car payments $_____

    Credit cards $_____

    Alimony $_____

    Loans $_____

    Other $_____

    Less Total $_____

    Total Income Available $_____

Credit History

YES   NO

❏   ❏   Do you have any foreclosures?

❏   ❏   Did you file bankruptcy in the past 10 years?

❏   ❏   Did you have any delinquent loans in the past 7 years?

❏   ❏   Did you have any late payments (where you paid a penalty) in the past 5 years?

❏   ❏   Do you know of any credit problems you may have?

☑ **FIGURE 14.1**
Buyer Qualification Chart (Continued)

Cash to Make Down Payment
The cash required to purchase this home including closing costs is $ _____

YES	NO	
☐	☐	Do you have this money in checking/savings?
☐	☐	Do you have it in another source such as a CD?
☐	☐	Are you borrowing it from relatives?
☐	☐	Will they co-sign the loan?
☐	☐	Are you borrowing it from a bank or other lender?

---

longer) that the borrowers may have. These include payments for cars, credit cards, alimony, and loans. If they're in debt up to their ears elsewhere, even with a high income, they may not be able to make your payments.

Ask for a Credit Report

After all, it's the minimum that any lender would demand. Be sure you get written permission from the buyers, or else it may be illegal for you to seek such information. You can get one through a real estate agent, or even directly through a credit bureau, with the buyers' permission. The three major national credit reporting bureaus are:

Experian	888-397-3742	<www.experian.com>
Trans Union	800-888-4213	<www.tuc.com>
Equifax	800-685-1111	<www.equifax.com>

If the buyers do have problems with a credit report, it may be that they have credit problems, and you want to get that into the open. If you're concerned that your buyers may be hiding some information, you can point out that every institutional lender will run a complete three-bureau credit check, which will reveal all of this information anyway.

What If My Buyers Answer Yes to Foreclosures and Bankruptcies?

Answering yes to any or all of the questions shouldn't automatically disqualify a buyer from getting a loan. Most lenders accept reasonable explanations—so should you. For example, a foreclosure may show up that was really for someone else with a similar name. In my own case, a foreclosed mortgage showed up for a property I had sold five years earlier. I simply presented my settlement papers for the deal, which showed that the buyer had assumed the mortgage when I sold the property and the foreclosure wasn't on my name, and the troubles went away.

However, if your buyers answer yes to the first two questions (foreclosure and bankruptcy) without having a good explanation, you could be in trouble. Most lenders simply won't consider them, so why should you?

What about Delinquencies and Slow or Missed Payments?

Delinquent loans and late payments are also undesirable but less condemning, if a good explanation is provided. For example, a bout of illness five years ago could account for late payments or delinquencies on a number of loans. However, if the borrower got well, made them all good, and has been current ever since, it's unlikely a lender would deny a mortgage because of the problem. Again, why should you?

However, what should you do if your buyers reveal a serious credit problem? My suggestion is that you state your doubts about their ability to make payments and, unless they can satisfy you with a reasonable explanation, forego giving them a loan.

What about the Buyers' Down Payment?

The final qualifying questions are designed to reveal the source of the buyers' down payment. You don't really care where they're getting it, as long as it isn't borrowed. The rule is that borrowed money should not be used as a down payment for the purchase of a home as it increases the total payments and it decreases the buyers' commitment to the property.

If the buyers put 20 or even 10 percent down, they will surely want to keep that property, if at all possible, out of fore-closure. But how serious will that commitment be if the buyers are putting in none if their own money?

What Kind of Financing Is Available?

Thus far we've been looking for a buyer who can afford to purchase your home. Now let's consider the types of financing that this buyer might obtain. You need to know a little about financing in order to talk intelligently to your buyer and steer him or her in the right direction.

All Cash to You

Essentially this means that the buyer gets a new first mort-gage from an institution such as a savings and loan association or a bank for a portion of the purchase price, typically 80 to 95 per-cent, and then pays cash for the balance of 20 to 5 percent. This is the ideal way to sell your home because you get all cash. (That's assuming, of course, that you want all cash. Some sellers prefer to get a portion of the sales price in the form of a mortgage. We'll cover that in the next section.)

You should be aware that for all conventional loans above 80 percent LTV (loan-to-value ratio), the borrower must pay an additional premium for private mortgage insurance (PMI), which protects the lender against default. This adds to the borrower's payments. (For FHA loans, this premium is usually built into the loan itself.)

Seller-Assisted Financing

We've already touched on how to qualify a buyer for seller financing. Now let's move into some of the advantages and pit-falls in offering such financing to your buyer.

For most sellers, a perfect world would see all buyers pay cash. In the real world, most buyers simply don't have enough cash for the down payment. Thus, buyers may ask you to assist them in making the purchase.

Should you assist with seller financing? The answer often comes down to something as simple as this: To make the sale, you may have to help with the financing.

You may find that you get lots of lookers trafficking through your property. Some are real buyers who would like to purchase, but no one seems to have the requisite cash and credit to make the purchase.

After a period of having your house on the market, you may decide that you have to do something to try to convert those would-be buyers to real buyers. That something is helping them with the financing. If they don't qualify for a full new mortgage, perhaps they'll qualify for part—and you can lend them the other part. If they don't have enough for a down payment, you can finance part of it.

Should You Offer a Second Mortgage?

The most common form of seller-assisted financing is the second mortgage. With this type of mortgage, instead of getting all cash you take back a mortgage for a portion of the sales price. For example, the buyers may have 5 percent cash to put down but can qualify only for an 85 percent mortgage, so you carry the remaining balance of 10 percent of the sales price.

85%	institutional mortgage
10%	second mortgage
5%	cash

There may be some advantages for you here. For example, you may get a relatively high interest rate, compared with sticking the same money in the bank. The bank may pay only 4 or 5 percent, but the second mortgage might pay 9 or 10 percent. That could mean a big return.

On the other hand, there are disadvantages. If the buyer defaults for any reason and doesn't make the payments, your only recourse might be to foreclose on your second mortgage and take the property back.

This can be an expensive proposition. The foreclosure process, depending on your state, can take from months up to almost a year. There probably will be back payments both on your second and on the first mortgage to make up during that time, plus taxes, insurance, and the costs of foreclosure.

In addition, once you get the property back, it may be in terrible shape and require a major fix-up.

My own feeling with regard to second mortgages is that if I help the buyer by providing one, I don't count it as money gained. Rather, I just forget about it. If the buyer pays regularly and eventually pays off, I regard it as a boon.

If the buyer doesn't make payments, I then have to decide whether it's worthwhile to foreclose. In some cases, I have simply forgotten the debt because the costs of foreclosure were too great. (Of course, in those cases I was able to sell for a high enough price that the second mortgage was gravy.) In other cases, foreclosure made sense. Prices had appreciated, the property came back, and after reselling, there was more profit to be made.

You must make a similar decision. If you're being asked to offer seller-assisted financing in the form of a second mortgage, you must decide whether the risk is worthwhile to you. If you are getting a high enough price, or if you're desperate to sell, you may go along with seller financing.

My suggestion remains, however: Don't think of it as money in the bank. The world of second mortgages is fraught with problems and pitfalls.

To help you estimate the actual risk involved, see Figure 14.2.

FACT

The more the buyer puts down in cash, the safer your second mortgage.

FIGURE 14.2   Evaluating Second Mortgage Risk

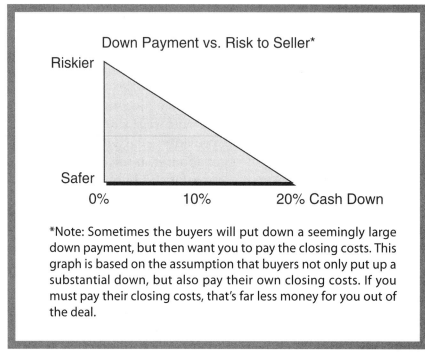

Down Payment vs. Risk to Seller*

*Note: Sometimes the buyers will put down a seemingly large down payment, but then want you to pay the closing costs. This graph is based on the assumption that buyers not only put up a substantial down, but also pay their own closing costs. If you must pay their closing costs, that's far less money for you out of the deal.

What about Nothing-Down Offers?

When you sell FSBO (and even when you have an agent!), you can expect to get all kinds of offers, many of which may be totally wacky. Unless you are careful, you may not recognize the bad offers from the good. One of the most common offers you are likely to receive is the offer of no down payment at all.

Here the buyers not only offer you nothing down but may also want you to pay all of the closing costs. As an enticement, these buyers may offer you full price, or even higher.

The seller who accepts such a nothing-down offer is usually one who is blinded by price and overlooks the reality of the deal. Remember, buyers who put no cash into a deal have no strong commitment to make monthly payments or to keep up the property. Such buyers may simply be out to resell for a profit as soon as possible.

If the market is going up and they are able to resell, you could come out okay. But if your buyers find that times are tough and they can't easily rent out the property, they'll keep the rent payments for themselves, and when you finally are forced to foreclose, just walk away.

Yes, this will taint their credit history, but some people may not care, and in any event, you would be stuck with trying to foreclose to get the property back. Not only would you have all the foreclosure costs mentioned earlier, but no cash down in your pocket to help offset them.

To my way of thinking, selling for no down payment is just asking for trouble. You are, in effect, delaying your current problem and making it worse. Your current problem is selling your home. By selling nothing down, you turn that problem over to someone who really doesn't care about you and who might dump the whole thing back in your lap in a few months, only with far more costs and expenses for you to bear.

Other Forms of Seller Financing

The second mortgage, although it is the most common form of seller financing, is not the only kind. If you own the property free and clear and if you want a steady income at an interest rate far higher than you could secure through a bank, certificate of deposit, or other similar vehicle, you might want to handle all the financing yourself by giving the buyer a first mortgage.

If you decide to offer a first, be sure that you go through the procedures a normal lender would. Insist on a credit report, verify income, and be sure the buyers put down at least 10 percent plus closing costs in cash.

Wraparounds

Another form of seller-assisted financing is called the *wraparound.* Here, you keep the existing first mortgage on your property yourself and the buyers pay you a single mortgage payment that includes the first and your second. In turn, you make the payments on the first and keep the balance for yourself. The wrap is fairly common in commercial deals where it is done with the consent of the lender. In residential deals, however, the lender is often not told. In fact, the whole point may be to circumvent the

due-on-sale clause in the first mortgage, which specifically pro-
hibits wraps.

Many sellers are tempted by the wrap, particularly because
it seems that they have greater control. They know when the payments are being made on the existing first mortgage. Further, it
may be the only offer they've recently received on their property.

The problem with the wrap, as noted above, is that it usually
breaks the terms of your first mortgage and puts you in jeopardy
of foreclosure. Most first mortgages today require you to pay
them off in full, if and when you sell the property. By wrapping
around the first, you don't tell the lender of the sale and hope to
continue making the payments and to keep the mortgage.

However, as soon as you record the sale, notice is usually
given to the lender of the first mortgage. Many times sellers hope
and pray that the lender of the first simply doesn't pick up the notice of sale. (Many times the lender won't!)

The risk, however, is that if the lender does, you could find
yourself being foreclosed upon and could ultimately lose all of
your interest in the property. (Your alternative would be to negotiate with the lender or to get a new loan—which is quite difficult
if you've already sold your house to someone else!)

To avoid this, sellers sometimes won't want to record the
sale. If you do this, chances are that the lender will never find out
you've sold the property. However, the buyer has no real protection that you won't resell it to someone else. For this reason, most
buyers will insist on recordation.

If wraps seem confusing and dangerous, it's because they
are. Unless you have really sound advice to the contrary from
your own real estate agent or attorney, I'd suggest that you stay
away from wraps.

Lease Option

In a lease option, instead of selling, you rent out your home
to a potential buyer on a long-term lease, usually for a couple of
years. The buyer often pays a higher rent with a portion of it to
be applied in the future to a down payment. The buyer has the option of eventually purchasing the property. You can often get the

majority of your money out by refinancing on your own before lease-optioning.

If you get a lot of option money up front, say 5 percent of the total purchase price, if the buyer continues to make payments on time, and if the buyer eventually purchases, the lease option can be an excellent method of selling a property.

However, a lot of the time the tenant/buyer doesn't want to put up much option money, perhaps none. Often, the tenant/buyer, after perhaps half the term of the lease, discovers he or she won't really be able to buy, and begins paying late, lets the property go, and eventually abandons it. Sometimes, in the worst case, the tenant/buyer won't pay and won't leave, and you have to initiate eviction proceedings. The eviction is made more difficult because the option, at least in theory, gives the tenant/buyer some slight ownership interest in the property. It could take you longer and it could be more expensive to evict under a lease option than under a standard lease.

I have had arguments with other real estate professionals who are proponents of lease options. They always seem able to point to cases where it has worked out beautifully. I, on the other hand, have seen too many cases where it has not.

My suggestion is to be very careful with the lease option and remember that it's not a sale. It's converting your home-for-sale to a rental with a hoped-for sale sometime in the future.

THE BEST RULE I HAVE FOUND

Never assist with financing unless the buyer agrees to an arm's-length purchase, puts at least 10 percent down, and pays in cash for the majority of the closing costs. You might lose some sales by insisting on this. But the one you make is more likely to stick.

15

Dealing with Disclosure

Most sellers are fearful when it comes time to deal with disclosure. They are afraid that when they let the buyers know things that are wrong with their property, they'll lose the deal.

Don't worry. The disclosure statement is actually the seller's friend. It helps protect you from the buyers coming back after the deal and demanding that you correct some deficiency in the property. If that happens, you can hold up the disclosure and say, "I told you all about it, yet you bought the property anyway! You have no gripe coming now."

Why Have Disclosure?

It all has to do with seller's liability. Just a few years ago the rule was "buyer beware." It was up to the buyer to determine any defects in the property. As a seller, you could sit back smugly and sell a pig in a poke, knowing that you were unlikely to have repercussions.

That's not true anymore. Litigation in many states has led to the concept that the seller has a duty to inform buyers of any known (and many unknown!) defects in the property. If you, as a seller, don't disclose the problems with the property, when you sell, it's possible, even likely, that the buyers could come back later on and claim to have been deceived. They could even sue for damages and, conceivably, for rescission (which means that you would have to take back the house and give back the buyers' money). While these dire consequences are unlikely, they have happened.

As a result of disclosure concerns, most states have instituted compulsory disclosure laws. Sellers in those states must disclose defects upon sale. Even if your state doesn't yet require it, it's still a good idea to disclose any defects in your property on your own.

Irwin's Theory of Disclosure

The way I see it, disclosure actually protects the seller more than the buyer. If you disclose a defect and the buyer moves ahead with the purchase knowing that the defect exists, it should strengthen your position. Perhaps an example will help.

I recently sold a property "as is" (meaning I would note defects, but not correct them) where there were significant cracks in the slab. It had not affected the liveability of the home, but I wanted the buyer to be aware that a problem existed.

In some parts of the country, a house is built atop a slab of concrete that is poured on top of the ground; there is no basement or crawl space area underneath. When slabs crack, those cracks are often reflected as cracks in the walls and ceilings as well. Typically, rebars (reinforcement steel bars) in the concrete hold the slab generally in position even if it cracks, but if the problem were to become severe, the floor conceivably could split with one spot being higher than another. It's usually, however, just an annoying problem. But a buyer who purchased a home unaware such a defect existed could be angry enough to seek redress.

Therefore, I gave the buyer a disclosure statement (described later on) on which I noted that there were cracks in the slab. Expansive soil underneath was unstable, particularly in wet weather when it could cause additional cracking in the house. I also noted there were cracks in the walls and in the ceilings. In short, I gave the buyer every notice possible of the defect. Further, I suggested that the buyer should hire his own inspector to come in and check out the problems, which he did. The inspector noted the cracks as well, but indicated they were old and unlikely to cause further trouble.

The house was sold and everything seemed fine until later that winter when the area had an abnormally large amount of rain. The ground beneath the slab became soaked and expanded, as can be the case with clay soils. The old cracks enlarged and a few new ones appeared in the ceilings and walls. The furious buyer called wanting me to fix all the problems.

I tried to calm him down, then reminded him that I had informed him of the cracks in the slab, the problem with the soil underneath, and the cracks in the walls and ceilings. He said he didn't care; he just wanted me to make repairs and if I didn't, he would hire an attorney.

I told him that an attorney was a good idea and to ask one what his chances of recovery were. We ended the conversation on that note. It's been several years and I haven't heard from that buyer since.

The moral here is that I believe it's best to disclose everything. I have become known among associates as one who provides very extensive disclosure statements. My disclosures are highly detailed.

And why not? Most sellers erroneously fear that disclosing defects will cause the buyer to shy away. I have found that not to be the case. Most buyers who are sincerely interested in the property will accept defects, or will negotiate the price to compensate for them, or will work with the seller to correct them. More to the point, the property is what it is. If it has a defect, it's better that you get it out in the open than that the buyer discover it a few months later.

If you want to be extra careful, you can insist the buyer accept the house with the defect "as is." However, remember that selling "as is" does not relieve you of the responsibility to disclose defects.

What about Defects I Don't Know About?

Changes in disclosure requirements have an added twist that would be comical if it weren't so serious. As a seller, you may be required to disclose defects in your home that even you don't know about!

For example, you could have a bad gas line leading to your hot water heater. You may not know about it, but if you fail to disclose it and later on, after a sale, there is a gas explosion in the property, you might be held responsible.

Incredible? The theory here is that as a seller it is up to you to investigate and discover most problems, certainly those involving health and safety, that involve your property and correct them as well as reveal them to the buyer.

In other words, to protect yourself, you should have a competent inspector look over the property before the sale to determine if there are hidden problems. Presumably, if the inspector gives you a clean bill of health, you're okay.

FACT

Most inspectors are great, but a few aren't. To protect themselves against complaints, many inspectors today include their own disclosure statement in their report saying they are not responsible for anything they don't find and, in some cases, even for things they do find! For more information, I suggest you look into my book, *The Home Inspection Troubleshooter* (Dearborn Trade Publishing, 1995).

Of course, this means that it's to your advantage to have an inspector check over your house. If anything happens later on, you can always point to the inspection and say that you made a good effort to determine any problems.

However, you probably won't have to pay for that inspection. Agents have worked hard to convince buyers that they need the inspection to uncover hidden defects that you, the seller, haven't disclosed. Therefore, most buyers are already primed to pay for an inspection (some states may even require it). All you have to do is insist on it and nine out of ten buyers are ready to pay for it. In reality, they are paying, in part, to relieve you of potential liability.

What Happens When the Inspection Uncovers Defects?

There's always the problem of defects that either you disclose or that the inspection uncovers and to which the buyer objects. For example, the inspection reveals that you don't have ground fault interrupter (GFI) plugs in your bathroom, which your local building code currently requires. (GFI plugs help prevent electric shock, but weren't required by most building codes until fairly recently.) Or the inspector notes that virtually all of the screens on your house's windows are old and decaying and should be replaced.

If it were my house, I would immediately replace the plugs with new GFI outlets. It's a matter of health and safety and it's simply a cost that I have to bear. (They cost about $10 apiece.)

On the other hand, screens are negotiable. The buyer wants me to replace the screens because it was in the inspection report, but I want a few extra days in which to move out. We compromise. I get my extra days; the buyer gets new screens.

When it comes to issues that don't involve health and safety, but that are negotiable, discuss them with the buyer. In most circumstances, you can reach a compromise.

By the way, money is a great compromiser. I was recently selling another home and a termite inspection revealed that a very large back deck was ruined by dry rot. The buyer wanted it replaced, at a cost of about $3,500 to me. Instead, I offered the buyer a reduction in price of $2,000 and acceptance of the deck as is. I pointed out that he could have the cash now, and later on as he had the opportunity, he could use the money to buy decking and rebuild the deck himself. He was quite happy with this arrangement.

How Do I Disclose Problems?

The simplest method of disclosure is to tell buyers about a problem as you show them the property. As you walk by the fireplace, for example, you note that it has a crack in the flue. The estimated cost of repair is $1,500, and it poses no health or safety hazard. You're prepared to take that off the price.

What you have to be particularly careful of, however, is documenting the disclosure. Yes, you may have fully explained the problem to the buyers, but six months later, when they claim you never told them, what do you have to back it up? If you have a disclosure statement describing the problem with their signatures on it, you're in much better shape.

F A C T

Give all disclosures in writing, dated and signed with acceptance by buyers.

When Should I Provide a Written Disclosure Statement?

The actual disclosure statement will vary enormously from area to area. In some parts of the country, no official disclosure statement exists and you will want to have your attorney draw it up for you. Figure 15.1 is an example of a typical disclosure statement. The question arises, however, of whether you should disclose all defects to the buyer up front or whether you should wait and disclose them after the buyer has signed a purchase agreement.

In California, which has some of the toughest disclosure laws in the country, a seller may give the buyer a written disclosure statement after the deal has been signed. However, the buyer then has three full days to rescind the deal by refusing to approve the disclosure with no penalty (no loss of deposit) for virtually any reason.

In purchasing property, some shrewd buyers have taken advantage of this California state law to make deals and then continue shopping around, knowing they have a full three days to back out without penalty. As a consequence, wise sellers give the disclosure statement to the buyer as soon as the deal is made. (Remember, you want the buyer to sign an acknowledgment that he or she has actually received the statement.)

FIGURE 15.1
Sample Disclosure Statement

THE FOLLOWING STATEMENT MAY NOT BE SUITABLE FOR USE IN YOUR STATE OR LOCALE. TAKE IT TO A LOCAL ATTORNEY OR REAL ESTATE AGENT AND ASK HIM OR HER TO MAKE IT APPROPRIATE FOR YOUR STATE AND LOCALE AND FOR YOUR SPECIFIC TRANSACTION.

SELLER'S DISCLOSURE STATEMENT

(To be filled out by seller and given to buyer. Seller, use a separate page to explain any defects or problems with property.)

YES NO WATER

❏ ❏ Any leaks (now or before) in the roof?

❏ ❏ Around a skylight, at a chimney, door, window, or elsewhere?
Was the problem corrected?
How?
By whom?
When? _____ By permit? _____ Final inspection when?_____

❏ ❏ Does the house have gutters?
Condition?

❏ ❏ Does the house have downspouts?
Condition?

❏ ❏ Any drainage problems?
Explain
How corrected?

❏ ❏ Water directed away from house?

❏ ❏ Flooding or grading problems?

❏ ❏ Settling, slipping, sliding, or other kinds of soil problems?

❏ ❏ Any leaks at sinks, toilets, tubs, showers, or elsewhere in house?

❏ ❏ Public water? _____ Or well? _____
Date well pump installed? _____

❏ ❏ Low water pressure?

❏ ❏ Are you involved in a bankruptcy?

FIGURE 15.1
Sample Disclosure Statement (Continued)

YES	NO	TITLE
❑	❑	Are you in default on any mortgage?
❑	❑	Do you currently occupy the property?
❑	❑	Have you given anyone else an option lease or right of first refusal on the property?
❑	❑	Does the property have any bond liens?
❑	❑	Can they be paid off without penalty?
❑	❑	Are there any boundary disputes?
❑	❑	Any encroachments or easements?
❑	❑	Shared walls, fences, or other such areas?
❑	❑	Any areas held in common such as pools, tennis courts, walkways, greenbelts, or other?
❑	❑	Notices of abatement filed?
❑	❑	Any lawsuits against seller that will affect title?
❑	❑	Do you have a real estate license?
❑	❑	Is there a homeowners association to which you must belong?
❑	❑	Any current lawsuits involving the homeowners association?
❑	❑	Any covenants, conditions, and restrictions (CC&Rs) in deed affecting property?
❑	❑	Any easements or rights-of-way over property to public utilities or others?

STRUCTURE

❑	❑	Any cracks in slab?
❑	❑	Any cracks in interior walls?
❑	❑	Any cracks in ceilings?
❑	❑	Any cracks in exterior walls?

FIGURE 15.1
Sample Disclosure Statement (Continued)

YES NO STRUCTURE (Continued)

❑ ❑ Any cracks in foundation?

❑ ❑ Any retaining walls?
Cracked?_____ Leaning?_____ Broken?_____

❑ ❑ Any driveway cracks?

❑ ❑ Any problems with fences?

❑ ❑ Is house insulated?
Attic?_____ Walls?_____ Floor?_____

❑ ❑ Double-paned glass windows?

❑ ❑ Moisture barrier in areas below ground level?

❑ ❑ Sump pump? Where?
Why?

❑ ❑ Septic tank?
Active?_____ Abandoned?_____ Filled?_____

❑ ❑ Connected to sewer?

EQUIPMENT

❑ ❑ Central furnace?
Forced air?_____ Radiant/water?_____ Radiant/electric?_____
Other? In working condition? _____

❑ ❑ Room heaters? In working condition? _____
Type?
Location?

❑ ❑ Central air-conditioning? Installed date? In working condition? _____

❑ ❑ Room air conditioners? Location? In working condition? _____

❑ ❑ Furnace room vented?

❑ ❑ Temperature relief valve on water heater? In working condition? _____

❑ ❑ Spa?

❑ ❑ Pool?

FIGURE 15.1
Sample Disclosure Statement (Continued)

YES   NO   EQUIPMENT (Continued)

❏   ❏   Pool heated?

❏   ❏   Cracks, leaks, or other problems with pool? Explain

❏   ❏   Any aluminum wiring?

HAZARDS AND VIOLATIONS

❏   ❏   Any asbestos?

❏   ❏   Any environmental hazards including, but not limited to, radon gas, lead-based paint, storage tanks for diesel or other fuel, contaminants in soil or water, formaldehyde?

❏   ❏   Landfill on or near property?

❏   ❏   Is property in earthquake zone?

❏   ❏   Is property in flood-hazard zone?

❏   ❏   Is property in landslide area?

❏   ❏   Is property in high fire-hazard area as described on a Federal Emergency Management Agency Flood Insurance Rate Map or Flood Hazard Boundary Map?

❏   ❏   Is property in any special study zone that indicates a hazard or requires permission to add to or alter existing structure?

❏   ❏   Are there any zoning violations pertaining to property? (Explain separately.)

❏   ❏   Were any room additions built without appropriate permits? (Explain separately.)

❏   ❏   Was any work done to electrical, plumbing, gas, or other home systems without appropriate permit? (Explain separately.)

❏   ❏   Does the property have an energy conservation retrofit?

❏   ❏   Any odors caused by gas, toxic waste, agriculture, or other?

❏   ❏   Were pets kept on the property? Type? _____ Inside? _____

❏   ❏   Are there any pet odor problems?

FIGURE 15.1
Sample Disclosure Statement (Continued)

YES   NO   HAZARDS AND VIOLATIONS (Continued)

❏   ❏   Are there any active springs on property?

❏   ❏   Any sinkholes on property?

❏   ❏   Is property adjacent to or near any existing or planned mining sites, toxic waste sites, or other environmental hazards?

❏   ❏   Is there any real estate development planned or pending in immediate area such as commercial, industrial, or residential development that could affect property values?

❏   ❏   Any abandoned septic tank?

❏   ❏   Is a Home Protection Plan available to the buyer?

REPORTS THAT HAVE BEEN MADE

The seller notes that the following reports have been made and are available to the buyer:

❏   ❏   Structural

❏   ❏   Geologic

❏   ❏   Roof

❏   ❏   Soil

❏   ❏   Sewer/septic

❏   ❏   Heating/air-conditioning

❏   ❏   Electrical/plumbing

❏   ❏   Termite

❏   ❏   Pool/spa

❏   ❏   General home inspection

❏   ❏   Energy audit

❏   ❏   Radon test

❏   ❏   City inspection

FIGURE 15.1
Sample Disclosure Statement (Continued)

YES	NO	ITEMS THAT GO WITH THE PROPERTY
❏	❏	Window coverings
❏	❏	Floor coverings
❏	❏	Range
❏	❏	Oven
❏	❏	Microwave
❏	❏	Dishwasher
❏	❏	Trash compactor
❏	❏	Garbage disposal
❏	❏	Bottled water
❏	❏	Burglar alarm system
❏	❏	Gutters
❏	❏	Fire alarm
❏	❏	Intercom
❏	❏	Electric washer/dryer hookups
❏	❏	Sauna
❏	❏	Hot tub
❏	❏	Spa
❏	❏	Pool
❏	❏	Central heating
❏	❏	Central air
❏	❏	Central evaporative cooler
❏	❏	Water softener
❏	❏	Space heaters

FIGURE 15.1
Sample Disclosure Statement (Continued)

YES NO   ITEMS THAT GO WITH THE PROPERTY (Continued)

❏ ❏   Solar heating

❏ ❏   Window air conditioners

❏ ❏   Sprinklers
           Where?

❏ ❏   Security gates

❏ ❏   Television antenna

❏ ❏   TV cable connections

❏ ❏   TV satellite dish

❏ ❏   Attached garage

❏ ❏   Detached garage

❏ ❏   Water heater
           Gas _____ Electric _____

❏ ❏   City water supply

❏ ❏   Public utility gas

❏ ❏   Propane gas

❏ ❏   Screens on windows

❏ ❏   Sump pump

❏ ❏   Built-in barbecue

❏ ❏   Garage door opener
           Number of remote controls _____

❏ ❏   Is the property equipped with smoke detectors?

FIGURE 15.1
Sample Disclosure Statement (Continued)

YES   NO   ITEMS THAT ARE SPECIFICALLY EXCLUDED FROM THE SALE

❏   ❏   Window coverings _____
          Where?

❏   ❏   Other Items
          Explain

❏   ❏   Lamps _____
          Where?

SELLER IS AWARE OF THE FOLLOWING DEFECTS AND/OR MALFUNCTIONS AND SPECIFICALLY DRAWS BUYER'S ATTENTION TO THEM:

BUYER IS ENCOURAGED TO MAKE A PHYSICAL INSPECTION OF THE PROPERTY AND TO EMPLOY THE SERVICES OF A COMPETENT INSPECTION COMPANY TO OBTAIN AN INDEPENDENT VERBAL AND WRITTEN REPORT OF THE PROPERTY'S CONDITION.

SIGNED BY SELLER AND BUYER

_____

_____

Handling Home Inspections

These days every buyer wants a home inspection, and some states even require them. Buyers want to look in every nook and cranny of your home and then often come back and demand that you fix this and that. As a result, sellers have come to dread the inspection process.

In reality, however, a home inspection protects you, the seller, as we'll shortly see. And there are ways to avoid expensive fixes that buyers may demand.

In this chapter, we'll examine:

- What a home inspection is
- Why you should go along on an inspection
- How to get second opinions
- How to write escape clauses in your contract

What Is a Home Inspection?

Inspections inform the buyer of any possible defects in the property. There are a variety of inspections that are typically performed these days. They include:

- Whole house
- Termite and pest (required by most lenders)

- Roof
- Soils
- Structural
- Pool and Spa
- Any other area of concern

From a buyer's perspective, a professional whole house inspection is valuable because it avoids the problem of buying a "pig in a poke." The buyer learns exactly what the condition of the property is. If something troubling is discovered, then typically the buyer will want an additional inspection of roof, soils, structure, or whatever else he or she feels is necessary. (A termite inspection is handled separately by a licensed pest inspector.)

FACT

Condition affects price. A home in perfect condition might be worth $300,000. However, if the roof is bad, the foundation cracked, and the pool leaking, the value would be significantly less. A home inspection helps the buyer determine value based on condition.

Why Would a Seller Want a Home Inspection?

The reason has to do with a recent change in the laws in most states. In the past, the buyer was at risk in a sale; it was up to the buyer to find out any defects with the property.

That's all changed. As we discussed in Chapter 15, today, litigation has favored the buyer to the point that now it's frequently up to the seller to disclose problems, even those problems that the seller may not know!

The result is that sellers encourage buyers to have inspections. If the buyer orders the inspection, it tends to put the seller in a more solid position so that later on the buyer can't easily come back and claim to have bought a defective home. The seller can say, "I opened my home to you. You hired a professional inspector. If he or she couldn't find the problem, how could I have been expected to know about it?!"

F A C T

A home inspection does *not* relieve the seller of disclosing any known defects. Rather, it helps to uncover defects unknown to the seller.

On the other hand, if a buyer declines to obtain an inspection, he or she likewise can't easily come back later, because then you will say, "I told you to get it inspected. You chose not to; hence, you shouldn't complain."

F A C T

Typically, a buyer pays for the home inspection.

What to Get Out of the Inspection

Normally, the inspection is requested in the purchase agreement. Indeed, most agreements today have language included which calls for an inspection. You should watch out for at least three things to protect yourself:

1. *Time limit.* Typically, it's 14 days. You give the buyer two weeks to obtain and approve an inspection report. Don't give longer unless there are unusual circumstances, otherwise the buyer can simply delay the purchase.

2. *You get a copy with the right to show it to others.* This is critical for two reasons. The first is that you want to see what was found. Second, if this deal doesn't go through, you should show subsequent buyers the report.

3. *Refusal right on work required.* You want to be able to choose whether and how to perform any repair work required. You don't want it to be automatic. For example, the report might conclude that your house needs a new roof at a cost of $15,000. You want to be able to decide whether to get a new roof, fix the existing roof, or simply not sell.

Who's the Inspector?

Because the buyer pays for the inspection and because it's the buyer who wants to discover problems, the buyer normally chooses the inspector. It's important to let the buyer do this. You don't want that buyer coming back and saying the inspector was biased because *you* chose him or her.

However, that doesn't mean that you should assume the inspector is all-knowing. He or she may range from expert to novice.

FACT

In very few states are home inspectors licensed today. In most states, anyone can hang out a shingle and call themselves a home inspector.

You should ask if the inspector belongs to a trade organization. There are two major national organizations: ASHI (American Society of Home Inspectors—www.ashi.com) and NAHI (National Association of Home Inspectors—www.nahi.com).

You should also ask if the inspector has any special training. Having previously been, for example, a county building inspector may uniquely qualify a person to be a professional home inspector. On the other hand, having previously simply been a carpenter may not. People with advanced credentials, such as structural or soils engineers, often also make excellent home inspectors.

Should I Go Along on the Inspection?

Yes, certainly. You have every right to go. And there are at least two advantages to doing so.

First, if a problem is found, you can ask the inspector firsthand to describe what it is and to suggest various remedies. You may learn far more this way than later on getting a dry written report.

Second, the inspector may think there's a problem where one does not exist. For example, the inspector may see water on a wall and conclude that there's a leak somewhere. You might be able to inform the inspector that your child had a party yesterday and you just washed the wall to get some marks off. You could head off a big problem by being there and helping the inspector avoid drawing incorrect conclusions.

A side benefit is that you can learn a whole lot about not only your house, but about the way homes are constructed and what to watch out for. This could help you when you buy your next home.

Anticipate that the buyer will also come along, but don't be surprised if he or she doesn't. Most buyers simply don't make the time to go with the inspector and, as a result, miss out on a lot of information that you'll get by being there.

What If the Inspector Finds Something Wrong?

Inspectors usually do. It's what they are paid to do. However, if the home is relatively new, the problems are usually minimal. Often they are nothing more than a broken light switch or a missing smoke detector.

If the report turns up items that total less than $100, don't even blink an eye. Either fix them or deduct the amount from the purchase price. It's when the report turns up something costing thousands of dollars that you need to pay special attention.

When serious money is involved, follow these six steps:

1. Be sure you understand exactly what the inspector's report says. If it says the roof is leaking, that doesn't necessarily mean you need a new roof. It may mean you need to fix a leak. The difference is around $10,000 or more for a new roof and a couple of hundred dollars for a fix.

2. If the inspection says that something must be replaced (such as the roof), demand a second opinion. Get a roofer out there, or two, or even three. Ask for alternatives to a whole roof replacement. Will a patch do?

3. If it turns out that the expensive item must indeed be replaced, offer to share costs with the buyer. For example, a roof typically will last 25 years. If you've only lived in the house for the past 10, why should you pay for a whole new roof? Offer to pay a third. If the buyer balks, go for half.

4. Offer a cash payment to the buyer (in the form of a price reduction) to remedy a problem. That's the cleanest. If the buyer refuses and insists that the work be done prior to closing escrow, demand that you select who does the work. Then get at least three estimates. You may find the prices differ enormously. If the buyer gets to select who does the work, you can be sure he or she will pick the highest bidder. If you get to select, you have the option of choosing the lowest.

5. If the issue is a health or safety concern, fix it. Don't refuse to fix a broken window or step. The buyer falling or cutting himself or herself in the first week could result in a lawsuit you don't want.

6. Do the work yourself, if you can, but only if it doesn't involve electrical, gas, or plumbing. The liability is too great. Also consider how good a job you'll do. Remember, it has to look good for the buyer to approve it.

Some problems can't be avoided, particularly if your house is older. You may have simply not kept up with maintenance and now it's come back to haunt you. It may just be the case that to sell your house (to this buyer or to *any* buyer), there is some work you need to do. If that's the case, then you'll have to bite the bullet and pay the costs.

What If the Buyer Demands a Large Price Reduction?

Some buyers purposely hope that the professional home inspector will find something big wrong. They can then parley this into a hammer to use to beat your price down. What should you do if you run up against this type of buyer?

Keep a cool head. Just remember that if you put the proper escape clause into your sales agreement noted earlier (you have the right to refuse to do any work), you're okay. You always can simply refuse to do the work.

Of course, this may mean that the buyers will walk. For example, if the heating system is shot and it costs upwards of $4,000 to fix and you refuse to pay for it, the buyers would be well within their rights to dump the deal and move onto the next home.

F A C T

Savvy buyers will always include a statement in the purchase agreement that says they have the right to approve or disapprove of the professional home inspection. And if they disapprove, they have the right to walk away from the deal with no strings attached, and get their deposit back.

Evaluate what the buyers are demanding. Is it reasonable? To get back to our roof example, say your roof is indeed shot and must be replaced. Are they reasonably asking for a replacement roof just like the one you have? Or do they want an upgrade to tile or cement costing thousands more?

Do the buyers actually want the problem fixed, or are they looking for a price reduction instead? Maybe they are willing to live with the problem, if you'll reduce the price.

Make a counteroffer. Insist on an apple-for-apples repair, and demand to only pay part of it, as noted above. Or offer a price reduction, but make it much less than the buyers want.

If the buyers are unwilling to compromise, then perhaps you'll want to walk. Sometimes the buyers are so determined on "stealing" your property that they're unwilling to agree to a reasonable compromise. If that's the case, then simply bailing out of the deal may be your best strategy.

If you stick to your guns and refuse to budge, either the buyers will back down, in which case you'll get a good deal, or they'll leave, in which case you'll avoid a bad deal.

The Bottom Line

Remember, a home inspection protects you as well as the buyer. There is really nothing to fear from it. The condition of your home *is* its condition. The inspection doesn't make it worse or better, it only reveals it. And if there are problems, you simply have to deal with them. Better to discover trouble early on, and cure it when you have options, then after the sale when the buyer's attorney comes knocking.

17

Controlling the Final Walk-Through

It has become common practice to offer buyers an opportunity to have a final look at the property just before closing escrow. This final walk-through often takes place immediately before the buyers go to the escrow office to sign their loan documents and deliver their cash down payment and closing costs. This allows the buyers to confirm that the property is in the same shape as it was when they first saw it and that any agreed on repairs have, in fact, been properly done.

Why Have a Final Walk-Through?

Most sellers look at the final walk-through as a pain in the you-know-what. They see it as at best an opportunity for the buyers to nitpick and demand more things be done and at worst as an opportunity for the buyers to actually back out of the deal.

It can be both of those things, if not properly controlled. However, the real reason for having a final walk-through is to avoid serious problems *after* the sale is completed. It is based on the belief that "a stitch in time saves nine." If you can find a problem before the sale is completed, you have a much better chance of solving it cheaply and effectively than afterward.

What Sort of Problems Can Arise?

They can be almost anything. For example, let's say one of the conditions of sale is that you replace a moldy bathroom floor. Although you've done it, the buyers thought it would be replaced with tile and you've replaced it with less expensive linoleum. They are very unhappy.

If this discovery happens after the sale, the buyers may be faced with living with linoleum, or suing you. Some choose the latter course, which is a big problem for you, the seller. (Even if you win a lawsuit, your attorney fees can be staggering. If it goes to small claims court where no attorneys are involved, the judges often exercise a Solomon-like discretion splitting the decision between parties.)

On the other hand, if the discovery is made prior to closing the sale, you have an opportunity to deal with it directly. You still have possession (presumably) of the home. You can go back and put in tile. (You can even do it yourself at a nominal cost.) Or you can make a money concession to the buyers. In other words, you can come up with a solution that works, that is inexpensive, and that avoids later unpleasantness.

The types of problems that occur are many and sometimes are very surprising. Here is a list of five such problems I've encountered at a final walk-though:

1. The buyers claim that a chandelier (or other light fixture) was not the same one they originally saw.

   If you're going to switch fixtures, do it before *you begin showing your home to prospective buyers. Otherwise, the buyers will assume everything they see goes with the house. You can, of course, try to exclude items in the sales agreement, but that's likely to start a fight. What the buyers don't see, they won't want.*

2. The buyers claim that agreed on work was not done, not done in a workmanlike manner, or the wrong materials were used.

   Go back to the original sales agreement and see what it says. It may turn out that you have discretion about what to do, how to do it, or even whether to do it. If the buyers signed, then they are committed to move forward regardless. Inform them of the penalties (loss of deposit and a possible lawsuit) for failing to complete the transaction as agreed. On the other hand, if you agreed to do something and haven't done it, get it done or else you could face the same penalties!

3. The buyers claim the house is dirty.

   Buyers have a right to expect a reasonably clean home delivered to them. By the final walk-through you may have already removed your furniture and when that happens, almost always scratch marks on walls and floors that were hidden by the furniture show up. Point out to the buyers that you never intended to re-paint or scrub down the house. On the other hand, if you've thrown a few parties since the deal was made and haven't cleaned up after yourself, do it now.

4. The buyers claim something is broken that was working before.

   Normally you agree to deliver the property in good condition, as it was when you first showed it to the buyers. That usually means, unless excluded, no broken windows or screens, all appliances working, heater and air conditioner working, and so forth. If something is broken, you will need to fix it.

5. The buyers find all sorts of things wrong and say they want to back out of the deal.

   This is the most serious problem you can face at a final walk-through and we'll deal with it at length.

When the Buyer Wants to Back Out

Why, you may ask yourself, would a buyer want to back out of the deal, particularly so late in the transaction process?

There can be many reasons. I've seen buyers who at the last minute found another property they preferred. They desired to back out of the deal in order to get the other home.

In other cases, buyers simply never looked closely at the property. Now, when they are finally faced with the purchase of it and the need to move in, they discover they don't like it and want out.

In yet another case, buyers now take a good look at the neighborhood for the first time and decide that it's not what they wanted.

Or the buyers could have financial problems. Perhaps some money they were expecting didn't show up and they are afraid of committing to a big home purchase. Or maybe they have discovered a great investment opportunity and would rather plunk the money into that than into buying your house.

Or maybe you've made all sorts of changes to the house and they don't like what you've done and want out.

Regardless, all but the last reason given above are not acceptable. (If you've messed up by changing the house, you might lose the deal or might need to bring the house back into its original condition.)

When the buyers signed the sales agreement, they committed to completing the transaction providing all conditions of *sale* were met. It doesn't matter if they change their minds or if a better investment shows up or if they find a more suitable house. They are committed to going through with the deal. However, converting that commitment into actually getting them to move forward sometimes can be a difficult thing.

What Does the Sales Agreement Say?

It all goes back to what you and the buyers originally agreed to. Usually the sales agreement will specify that the buyers have the right to conduct a final walk-through. But the devil is in the details. What are the specifics of this right? (This is another reason you want an attorney or a good real estate agent to draw up the sales agreement!)

Is the Walk-Through a Contingency of the Sale?

In some sales agreements, the language is something to the effect that buyers must give approval of final walk-through. What this is saying is that the purchase is contingent on the buyers' approval. If the buyers don't approve, there is no purchase. If language like this is in your sales contract, then the buyers may indeed have a way out, regardless of their motives.

On the other hand, some sales agreements that are tighter say that the buyers will have an opportunity to have a final walk-through for the purpose of inspecting work that was done and determining that the home is essentially the same as it was when they first saw it. Some also add a notice that specifically states the final walk-through is not for the purpose of giving the buyers a new opportunity to decide whether or not to purchase.

This type of language makes it much more difficult for buyers to back out of the deal. The only arguments here should be over how work was done and whether there were any significant changes to the property between the time the buyers first made their offer and the final walk-through.

These are usually demonstrable sorts of things and can be settled, as noted earlier, by redoing work, by cleaning, or by replacing items. In other words, it should be possible to satisfy any of the buyers' reasonable demands and demonstrate that any unreasonable demands are, well, unreasonable.

Here buyers who want to back out for hidden motives are faced with dealing with an angry seller who might just keep their deposit and even take them to court for "specific performance" (forcing them to complete the purchase or pay a mover penalty).

Will the Right Language Keep You Out of Trouble?

Not necessarily, but as we've seen, it should help. And remember, have an attorney or a good real estate agent write up the sales agreement so that it contains the language you need.

How Much Should You Bend?

We've seen two extremes. In one case, the buyers were justified in their demands made after the final walk-through. In the other, they were not.

But sometimes there's a gray area in between. For example, you agree to replace a rotting deck. You do the work and then stain the wood a redwood color.

The buyers come for the final walk-through and are dismayed. They wanted a light cedar stain. They want you to change the color.

Changing the stain on wood is not so easy. After all, stain goes *into* the wood. To change could mean sanding the wood down or even replacing it and staining again—not something you'll want to do.

So, what's to be done here?

If it were me and the buyers had reasonably conveyed to me the color they wanted and I had forgotten or got it wrong, I would make a money concession. Perhaps knock a few hundred dollars off the price. Explain to the buyers that by next year the wood will again need restaining and then they can get the cedar color they want. They might not be entirely satisfied, but it's a reasonable concession and will most likely be accepted.

On the other hand, if the buyers never expressed any color preference, and particularly if the previous deck was redwood stained, I would make no concession whatsoever. I would stick to my guns, note that the new deck was stained the same as the old, and demand the buyers continue with the purchase. More than likely they would, although again they might not be happy about it.

Only if this became such an incredibly big issue that the buyers were willing to risk losing their deposit and the sale would I consider a concession, just to complete the transaction. And then only a small one! I might simply say, "Okay, I don't owe it, but here's a hundred bucks and let's finish the deal." Sometimes people just want to be right and it's easier to let them have their way than to get into a hassle.

THE RULE TO FOLLOW

The general rule is that you should keep your eye on the doughnut and not the hole. Your goal is to sell your house. If things get bogged down at any point, here in the case of the final walk-through, do what's reasonable in order to get things back on track.

18

Tax Consequences of Selling

Will you need to pay taxes on the sale of your home?

Probably not. But a lot depends on how long you lived there and how big your profit was.

If your net selling price is more than your tax base (usually what you paid for the property), the difference is called a capital gain and tax may be owed on it.

That would certainly be the case if the property were a rental or investment property. But what if it's your home? Is there still a capital gains tax?

There may be, but you may not have to pay it. A different set of rules applies to principal residences. Provided you meet the criteria, you can exclude a very large portion of your gain from taxes, up to $250,000 a person ($500,000 for a married couple).

If you qualify, you can take the money and run–that is, sell your home and pocket the profit without paying taxes on it.

Sound too good to be true? This is one case where it really is true. Of course, the catch is qualifying and that's what we'll consider in this chapter.

NOTE

The following tax discussion should be considered an overview of an extremely complex subject. Be aware that the tax laws are in a constant state of flux, being changed by Congress, the courts, and IRS interpretations. What you read here today may not be true tomorrow. Therefore, before taking any action with tax consequences, consult a competent tax professional.

What Is the Exclusion?

The Taxpayer Relief Act of 1997 provides an exclusion of up to $250,000 per person on the sale of a primary residence, or up to $500,000 when a married couple filing jointly sell their home.

For example, let's say that your capital gain is $400,000. As a married couple filing jointly and otherwise qualifying, there's no tax to pay.

On the other hand, if you're a qualifying single person with a $400,000 gain, the first $250,000 is excluded. You pay taxes on the remaining balance of $150,000.

There Are Many Benefits and Requirements

You can take advantage of this tax exclusion repeatedly, up to once every two years. If you sell and buy a primary residence today, then two years from today you can sell that new house and claim the exclusion all over again. You can claim the full exclusion as many times as you want, as long as you own and reside in each house for a minimum of two years.

Further, you don't need to invest that money in another house. You can use it any way you want: to buy a boat or a car, take a vacation, or blow it in Vegas. It's your money to do with as you wish.

The two-year qualifying period does not have to be continuous. The rule is that it must be the previous two out of five years. Thus, as along as you can come up with 24 months out of the previous 60 during which you actually lived in the property and otherwise qualify, you can take the exclusion.

In some cases, you don't even have to live in the home for the qualifying two-year period. A seldom talked about part of the new tax law provides that if you change the location of your employment, a health condition requires you to sell, or an unforeseen circumstance occurs that mandates the sale, you may not be required to have kept the home for the full two-year period. While the interpretation of this part of the law is in a gray area, it appears that it is quite liberal. A wide variety of reasons may be acceptable for an early sale. Check with your accountant or tax attorney.

Further, the amount of the exclusion you can claim under this provision, as of this writing, appears to be $\frac{1}{24}$ for each month you actually lived in the property. In other words, if you lived in the property for only 12 months, you'd get half, or up to $125,000. It's the rare house whose value increases that much that quickly. As I indicated, check with your tax professional for more details.

Should I Watch the Time Frame Closely?

If you anticipate selling your home FSBO in the near future, it would be wise to first spend some time with a tax consultant to determine the optimum time for selling. It might turn out that you don't qualify for the exclusion noted above because you haven't lived in the home two out of the previous five years. In that case, maybe you'd want to live there for an additional time to be sure that you qualify.

Further, you'll want to determine what, if any, your capital gain will be. (After all, if it's a tiny amount, you may not care if you have to pay taxes on it.) The capital gains calculation requires that you apply a fairly rigorous set of calculations to the monies you anticipate from the sale (check with your accountant). It may be that after improvements to the property that you've made are added in, you have little to no capital gain. Or if your property is in a rapidly appreciating area, perhaps the gain is huge. Depending on the calculation and the time frame, you may want to hold off on the sale—or move forward with it even more quickly!

The Home Must Be Your Principal Residence

What is a principal residence? To qualify for the exclusion, the property must be your main home, where you live most of the time. The government gives a lot of leeway as to what that means. Your principal residence can be your house, condo, or other type of home. A trailer home has been considered a personal residence as has a house boat!

It's important to understand, however, what principal residence really means. It has to be where you reside most of the time. It has to be truly your home.

A lot of confusion occurs with regard to rentals. Can a rental be a personal residence? Obviously, for purposes of the exclusion, if you're the tenant, the answer is no.

But what if you're the landlord? Let's say that you own a duplex (or duet as it's called in some parts of the country) and live in one side while you rent out the other. Is the duplex your principal residence?

Yes and no. Strictly speaking, only half of it is. The part in which you reside is your principal residence. The part that you rent out is investment property. For purposes of the exclusion, half of any gain should be subject to the rule, while the part of the gain coming from the rental side should be subject to capital gains taxes in the year the property is sold.

What happens if after living in your home for many years, you move and rent it out. Later you decide to sell. Is it still your principal residence? This was a gray area in the past, but the new rule has helped to clear it up. Remember, you only had to live in the property for two out of the previous five years. That means you could have rented the property out for three of those years.

On the other hand, if you rented it out for four of the previous five years, you're probably out of luck.

Should you move back in before selling? It's something you may want to consider, depending on your situation. If you've rented it out for too long to qualify for the two out of five year provision, you may want to delay the sale and move in until you do qualify.

What about claiming you lived there? As we all know, anything can be claimed. I suspect, however, that the Internal Revenue Service isn't likely to look favorably on a less than legitimate claim. If you have rented out the property for more than three years, you probably will be challenged as to whether you meet the requirement.

If the Gain Is Much Higher Than the Exclusion, Can Part of It Be Rolled Over?

The new law is great if you don't make too much money on the sale of your home. But it's not so great for those relatively few homeowners who have huge profits.

In the old days (before the 1997 law went into effect), you could roll over or defer the payment of capital gains taxes provided you bought a replacement house within two years. The amount you could roll over was unlimited.

However, the new law did away with the rollover provision. If your gain is more than the maximum exclusion, then you'll end up paying tax on everything above the limit. You can't roll over the excess into a replacement home.

The Exclusion Applies Only to Your Capital Gain

This is an important point because many sellers confuse what they consider profit with a capital gain. Capital gain is a very specific figure that must be determined in a manner prescribed by the tax code and enforced by the Internal Revenue Service.

Your capital gain is basically the sales price less most costs of sale less your basis in the property (usually what you paid for it increased by improvements and other items and decreased by depreciation, if any, and other items). In other words, if you paid

$100,000 including costs for the property, that is probably your basis. If you later sell for $150,000 after most costs of sale, your capital gain will be around $50,000.

Sound simple?

Sometimes it is, sometimes it isn't. As noted earlier, I would strongly suggest that unless you're very familiar with the tax code, you do not try to determine your capital gain yourself. It's worth the few dollars required to have a certified public accountant do it right.

What Happened to the Once-in-a-Lifetime Exclusion for Those Aged 55 and Older?

Under the old rules, you were allowed to exclude up to $125,000 once in a lifetime after age 55, provided other conditions were met. The new up to $250,000/$500,000 exclusion does away with the old rule. You can take the new exclusion as many times as you want (providing you meet the two out of five year minimum stay requirement). You can take it at any age. You no longer must wait until you're 55.

Do State Laws Reflect the Federal Tax Code Changes?

It's important to understand that the federal tax code changes only apply to federal income tax. Each state decides whether to change its own tax code.

Most states have reworked their tax codes to match or at least be similar to the federal changes. However, don't assume that what works for the Feds will automatically work for the state. You may be responsible for taxes under two sets of tax codes (federal and state). You might be able to exclude at the federal level, but still owe taxes (or perhaps be able to roll them over) at the state level. Be sure to consult your accountant.

What If I Have an Office in My Home?

The new tax code and subsequent changes affects home offices in two ways. First, it expanded the opportunity for a home office by making the requirement that you do most of your business at the home more lenient. However, the other rules still apply, mainly that the space must be used exclusively for business purposes and that the business actually be viable (not just a hobby). There are other requirements for a home office that are beyond the scope of this book—check with your accountant.

Second, it changed the way in which depreciation taken for a home office is handled. If you are using a portion of your home as an office at the time you sell, that portion does not qualify for the up to $250,000 exclusion. In other words, just like splitting up a duplex into the portion you lived in and the portion you rented out, you'd have to split up the home as part residence and part business, and the business part doesn't qualify for the exclusion.

Further, if you took depreciation on your home office at some time in the past, you may be required to recapture that depreciation. In other words, the depreciation you took may now be taxed at a special capital gains rate.

Obviously, this entire subject is complex. Here again, be sure to consult a tax professional on your options and your tax liability if you've ever had an office in your home.

19

Step-by-Step
to Closing

Finding buyers and getting them to sign a sales agreement may seem like the hard part. But even after you've done that, there is still one more hoop that you must jump through, and that is closing escrow. Closing involves doing everything necessary to make escrow complete, to get all the money into escrow that is required to purchase the property and to provide clear title for the buyer.

Unfortunately, most FSBO sellers don't worry much about this closing, believing instead that it's all over once the sales agreement is signed with the buyers. In truth, that may just be the beginning.

Step-by-Step to Closing

Once you've found a buyer and gotten a signed sales agreement, it normally takes anywhere from as little as 30 days to as long as 90 days to close the deal. Along the way, you have a lot of problems to solve and tasks to perform. (See Figure 19.1.)

FIGURE 19.1
Steps in the Closing Process
(Short 30-Day Escrow)

FIRST WEEK
- Sales agreement is signed.
- Buyer applies for mortgage.
- Escrow is opened and deposit inserted.

SECOND WEEK
- Check with lender on mortgage application process.
- Title search is completed.
- Inspections are ordered.

THIRD WEEK
- Termite work and other repairs are done.
- Title problems (if any) are cleared.
- Lender gives buyer formal loan approval.

FOURTH WEEK
- Buyer does final walk-through.
- Buyer signs loan documents.
- Seller signs off title.
- Deal closes.

Your First Week

If you were working with an agent, that person would now do the grit work, those unexciting but absolutely necessary jobs that must be done. These include the following:

Be sure that the buyer applies for a mortgage. I always list this first because without a mortgage, you won't have a deal. (You may have a better chance of winning a state lottery than of finding an all-cash buyer.) Although you can't normally walk the buyers to a lender, you can insert a clause in the sales agreement specifying that the buyers will immediately apply for a mortgage and if the buyers aren't fully preapproved, the lender will fully preapprove them and issue a commitment within a reasonable amount of time, say 7 to 14 days from the signing of the sales agreement.

F A C T

Full approval means that the lender has checked the buyers' credit and verified income and cash on hand and determined the buyers will qualify for the needed mortgage. The lender may then issue a commitment letter. This is different from a preliminary preapproval letter, which may not have gone through all of the above steps.

You can ask the buyers which lender they have gone through (see Chapter 14 on financing) and then check with that lender to see how the mortgage is progressing. Be aware, however, sometimes the lender will not talk directly to you, only to the borrower.

However, your safety valve is that final lender's commitment letter. If you don't get it within 7 to 14 days, you may want to return the buyers' deposit and start looking for a new buyer. (Note: In the past, it often took a full 30 days to get such a commitment from a lender. Today, electronic processing has dramatically shortened the response time.)

The reason for being strict here is that in the vast majority of cases, what makes the deal go through (title changes hands and you get your money) is having buyers who can get the necessary mortgage.

But what about that preapproval letter that the buyer initially showed up with?

Unfortunately, even with the preapproval letter that you received before you signed the sales agreement, you really don't know for sure that the buyers will actually be approved for a new mortgage. I have worked with buyers who, seemingly, had excellent credit only to find weeks into the deal that they had hidden a foreclosure or a bankruptcy or bad payments in another state. In one case, a buyer seemed to have enormous income; only later did it come out that he had to make huge alimony and child-support payments, which reduced the amount of his income that could be applied to the mortgage and thus disqualified him.

Open escrow. Most states now use escrow services for real estate transactions. These can be handled by an independent escrow company or an attorney, especially in those states where attorneys handle the closings.

Opening the escrow means that you take your signed sales agreement to the escrow officer and receive an escrow number. The escrow company, in conjunction with a title insurance company, now begins a title search to be sure that you can give the buyer clear title to your property. The escrow company also will draw up all the documents (with the exception of the loan documents, which will come from the lender) needed to complete the transaction. Because this all takes time, you want to immediately open escrow after signing the sales agreement.

Also, you will want to put the deposit money the buyer gave you into escrow. As noted earlier, the buyer is unlikely to trust you with this money. The easiest solution to this potential problem is to have the check made out to escrow, an independent third party.

Keep in mind, however, that if the deal doesn't go through and there is no language specifying what is to happen to the deposit in that event (see your attorney), the money will remain in escrow. It will go to neither you nor the buyer until you both agree on its disposition. (I've seen a deposit languish for months in escrow while the buyer and seller argued over who was to get what. It's best that you have your attorney handle this beforehand.)

Your Second Week

The approval/commitment letter of the buyer for a mortgage should have been issued. If it hasn't, you need to find out why not. It might turn out that your buyer can't qualify.

If the letter has been issued, don't think you're home free. Anything can happen between now and the time title changes hands. The buyer could lose his or her job. They could spend the down payment money elsewhere. Even the lender could go out of business!

A good rule of thumb is to not count on the deal closing until it's closed!

Get the preliminary title report. This should be issued by the second week. It will reveal any problems you may have on your title.

Don't smirk. You may have problems there you don't even know about. For example, someone may have filed a lien on your property in error. You may be totally innocent, but now you have to locate whoever filed that lien, convince him or her of the error, and have this party remove it. Sometimes you have to get an attorney to accomplish this.

Other problems could affect the title such as an encumbrance or easement that prevents you from getting clear title. It's up to you to identify the problem and solve it.

Order inspections. Another matter is the various inspections that may be needed. Almost certainly the lender will require a termite clearance before funding the loan. To get this, you (not the buyer) need to order a termite inspection. Also, the buyer may want a housing inspection, roofing inspection, or any of a dozen other kinds of inspections. (See Chapter 16 on inspections.) Normally the buyer orders these, but you will need to coordinate them so that the property is available to be seen when the inspector arrives.

Note: If for some reason the sale doesn't close, you will be responsible for paying the costs of any inspections you order. That is why I suggest waiting a week to see if the buyer gets that preliminary letter of qualification. At least then you have a better hope that the deal will close.

FACT

Usually the buyer will pay for the professional home inspection at the time it is done.

Your Third Week

By the third week you should be really rolling. The inspections should have been completed and required repairs noted. In addition, any credit problems the buyer has should have surfaced. If none has, the lender will set a date for funding the loan. This means that your buyer has the mortgage in the bag. (But be careful, as we'll see shortly, that bag could still have a few holes in it.)

Once the buyer has final loan approval (or earlier, as needed) you will want to authorize repair work. This may mean anything from fixing a broken window to tenting the house to remove termites. Just keep in mind that once the work is ordered, it must be paid for whether or not the deal closes, and usually you're the one to pay for it. For that reason, most sellers wait until the last possible moment before ordering the work done.

Finally, you should have cleared up any problems in the title. Mistaken liens and other title clouds will have been removed.

Your Fourth Week

By the fourth week in an ideal closing, the lender is ready to fund. The buyer may want a final walk-through. (See Chapter 17 for more details.) The buyer again looks at the house, mostly to see that it's in the same condition as when the sales agreement was signed.

Once the final walk-through is completed, the buyer will go to the escrow officer and sign all the loan documents as well as deposit the cash down payment and closing costs. The escrow officer will let you know when this has to be done. (Lenders usually leave a window of only a few days during which all the documents must be finalized.)

Once the lender has signed the documents, you need to sign the deed, as well as any additional escrow instructions.

And then you're done!

Now you wait.

You are waiting for the lender to fund the loan, then for the escrow officer to record the deed and mortgage and issue your check to you. If the deed is recorded in the morning, you can usually have your check the same day.

What If Problems Arise?

As the famed baseball star Yogi Berra was fond of saying, "It ain't over till it's over!"

What could possibly go wrong? Probably very little, but there's always something. The lender might not fund. The lender might have discovered a credit or income problem with your buyer at the eleventh hour—unlikely, but it could happen—or the lender might itself suddenly be immersed in financial problems and not have the funds needed. Also, someone might record a lien or other encumbrance affecting your title. Again it's unlikely, but it could happen.

If the unforeseen does happen, you'll simply have to deal with it. In most cases, the worst that will happen is a delay. It is possible, however, in a worst-case scenario, actually to lose the deal after everything is signed and before the deed has been recorded.

Longer Closings

What we've seen here is an ideal 30-day closing. Yours may take much longer. The need for extensive physical repairs may prolong the escrow, or a title problem could require an attorney and court action to eliminate, or the buyer may not be able to immediately get all the cash together, or anything else could happen. These days escrows of 60 and even 90 days are not uncommon.

Beware of losing the buyer's loan in a longer-than-anticipated escrow. Lenders often offer commitments to fund. This means that the lender guarantees a rate and points for a specified time. That time is rarely more than 45 days and usually is as little as 30 days. If the escrow takes longer, the lender may still fund, but not at the originally quoted interest rate or points. That means the buyers may no longer qualify.

FIGURE 19.2
Closing the Deal Checklist

Items You Need to Do

1. Be sure buyer applies for mortgage.

2. Insist on a 7- to 14-day approval/commitment letter.

3. Use signed sales agreement to open escrow and place buyer's deposit in it.

4. Order inspections.

5. Remove any title problems you may have.

6. Check on buyer's progress in getting mortgage.

7. Find out when mortgage will fund.

8. Order all work that needs to be done.

9. Do final walk-through.

10. Sign all documents.

Also, if interest rates have jumped up after the sales agreement was signed but before the escrow closes, it could cost your buyer more money and higher payments. He or she may not want to or be able to pay more. Depending on how the sales agreement was prepared, your buyer may be able to walk if interest rates rise above a ceiling. Or the lender may say that your buyer qualified at a lower rate but not at the newer, higher rate.

No, it's not likely to happen, but a longer escrow can bring its own set of problems. If I have the option, I always go for the shortest escrow possible.

Special Tips for Hard to Sell Homes

What if, in spite of your best efforts, you put your house up for sale FSBO and after a set time, say three months, it still doesn't sell? I'm sure this is a major fear in the backs of the minds of everyone considering selling FSBO.

If this happens to you, first and foremost, don't panic. Just get a cup of tea (or coffee), take a deep breath, and reflect. It's time to look at your alternatives. In this chapter, we'll discuss what to do if your property doesn't sell.

By the way, if you're one of those anxious people who turned to this chapter first, stop. Don't bother reading here because chances are you won't need this information. Go back to the beginning and keep an optimistic outlook.

Causes for a Home Not Selling

If you've given a FSBO sale your best shot and your home still hasn't sold, then you have to look for likely causes. There are five main reasons that a house doesn't sell (see Figure 20.1). Let's consider each separately.

FIGURE 20.1
Five Reasons a House Doesn't Sell

1. The resale market is bad.

2. Your house's location is poor.

3. Your price is too high.

4. Your house shows badly.

5. Your terms aren't competitive.

1. The Resale Market Is Bad

As of this writing, the residential resale market in most areas is quite healthy. However, that hasn't always been the case and may not be the case again.

In the 1990s, various parts of the country ran into a real estate recession with few buyers and declining prices. While it's beyond the scope of this book to go into the reasons for that downward trend in real estate, it is worth noting that like other markets, real estate is cyclical. It will have ups and downs over time. Therefore, I believe it's worth your while to determine the condition of the overall resale market in your area at the time you want to sell.

If you can't sell, it may simply be that nothing at all is selling. In other words, check with the local Board of REALTORS® to find out how many houses are selling per month in your area. If it's almost none, you immediately know what your problem is: the market in your area is severely depressed. If that's the case, consider some of the alternatives given later in this chapter.

2. Your House's Location Is Poor

Another reason for the inability to sell is a poor location. Factors making for a poor location include the following:

- An environmental hazard such as a dump site
- High-tension electrical wires
- A sewerage facility of some sort
- A noisy or smelly factory
- A particularly high-crime area
- A blighted neighborhood
- Other factors that would alienate buyers

While you may have taken this into account initially when you bought the property, perhaps you didn't give it enough weight. Regardless of how nice your particular house is, potential buyers may be shunning your area because of some nearby detrimental influence.

If this is the case, then the only realistic thing you can do is lower your price and/or offer more advantageous terms. If you had time, you could attempt to organize the neighborhood and seek ways to change the harmful influence, but that could take years. To attract buyers in the short run, you may simply have to make your house into more of a bargain.

3. Your Price Is too High

Even if you don't have a bad neighborhood influence, your home may still be priced too high for the local market to bear. Perhaps you didn't do as good a job of checking comparables as you thought. Remember, while for you checking the market is an academic exercise, for buyers it is an urgent and vital task. After a few days of looking at homes, buyers become attuned to what a house should sell for. If your home is even a few thousand over market price, they may shun it and not make offers.

Reexamine the comparables. For a weekend, pretend you're a buyer and visit every home for sale in your area around your price range. (Work with an agent on this.) Very quickly you'll see if you've priced yourself even a little bit too high.

Then you'll have to suck in your breath and take the plunge; lower your price accordingly.

4. Your House Shows Badly

Reexamine the appearance of your house, only don't take your own word on it. Seek the advice of experts. Contact two or three agents. (After having put up your home FSBO, you should have the names of dozens of agents who have contacted you.) Have them come over and tell them that you've had trouble selling FSBO. You're thinking of listing (which you undoubtedly are). Would they have any suggestions to make about the outside/inside presentation of your home?

You may be astonished at the suggestions offered. It may turn out that the wonderful shrubs that have lovingly grown over the years are hiding the front of your house and need to be hacked out. Maybe the entranceway that you painted lavender would look better in beige. Perhaps the tile you yourself laid in the front hall would be better if removed and a professional laid linoleum in its place.

The point is that you probably aren't able to see objectively what's wrong with the presentation of your property. If two or three others, however, all agree on some item that needs to be improved, consider doing the work. Once it's done, try again to sell FSBO. Removing the objection may result in hooking a buyer.

5. Your Terms Aren't Competitive

Although we've discussed this, often it's hard to really believe it. In a tight market, sometimes you simply cannot sell for cash. Cash-down buyers may not be out there. So to get a sale, you may have to offer low-down-payment financing and carry some of the paper yourself.

I know that getting cash out of your property is often the most advantageous method of selling. You know it, too, but if your choice is to sell with paper or not to sell at all, what are you going to do? Sometimes you have to compromise. Further, remember that a FSBO seller often has to go the extra mile to get that sale.

Your Other Alternatives

If you've considered the five main reasons for failure to sell noted above and have taken what corrective steps you can and still your property doesn't sell, what are your alternatives now?

List with a Full-Service Broker

My suggestion is that if you do your best as a FSBO seller and you still can't find a buyer after a set time, try listing. You can still list with a discount broker, as discussed in Chapter 5, or you can list with a full-service broker. You may want to go with the latter, if you've had a lot of trouble selling on your own.

Don't find yourself wedged into a corner by stubbornness. Don't fail to sell simply because you can't do it FSBO.

The key, of course, is the time limit. As I've made it a point to note, set a reasonable time limit, whether it's a couple of months or half a year. If you still have not sold after the time limit has expired, consider listing.

Take It Off the Market

Maybe no houses are selling in your area. The market could be terrible. So terrible, in fact, that you simply can't find a buyer either FSBO or through an agent.

If that's the case, consider hanging onto your property until times get better, which they surely will. This means that you may have to hold your property for a year or more. Ideally, you will be able to continue living in your property, working in the area, and making the payments. If you can do all of these, then you may simply want to defer selling for a while. Remember, when the market eventually does turn up, you will probably be able to sell quickly and, very likely, for more money.

Lease It

Maybe you can't sell, and you can't stay there. Perhaps you have to move because of a change in employment. Perhaps an illness requires you to get out from under that mortgage payment. If you can't stay and you can't sell, consider leasing the property.

Very often you can lease the property for at least your mortgage payment, and you may be able to write off your interest, taxes, insurance, and other costs as well as depreciation, which actually gives you a tax advantage at year end. (Note: Tax law changes restrict the ability to write off any real estate losses against personal income on an annual basis. Check with your accountant to see if you qualify.)

Leasing the property also carries risks. Tenants almost never treat the property as well as you would. There's bound to be some wear and tear in the best of situations and, if you get a bad tenant, there could be real damage as well as the costs of eviction. While this can happen, if you rent judiciously, it's less likely to. (I suggest you check into *The Landlord's Troubleshooter,* Dearborn Trade Publishing, 1999.)

Try a Lease Option

Yet another alternative is the lease option. Here you lease the property to a tenant and, typically, allow a certain percentage of the higher rent payment to apply toward a down payment when he or she eventually purchases. You have combined leasing with the potential for purchase.

Lease options become more favored during slumping real estate markets. However, their value is directly related to the tenant's eventually exercising the option and purchasing the property. If the tenant doesn't eventually buy, you will take back the property, often in poor condition because at the end of the lease-option period the tenant often resents the higher payment and takes it out on the property.

Studies have shown that the chances of the tenant's eventually buying the property improve in a direct relationship to the amount of the rent that goes to the option. For example, if the rent is $1,000 a month and $50 goes toward the option, the tenant is far less likely to buy than if $500 a month goes toward the option.

I personally have had mixed results with lease options, although I do know people who have had a lot of success. As a result, I simply cannot unconditionally recommend them.

Walk Away

Bad choice. In desperate situations, some sellers who can't sell (they may owe more than their property is worth), can't stay (their job may require a move to a different state), and can't lease (too many properties are for rent or for sale) simply walk away from their properties. They let the house go to foreclosure.

I don't recommend this practice—ever. A foreclosure ruins your credit rating. Although you may be able to establish enough credit to get a credit card in a few years, it could take a decade, if ever, before a lender is likely to give you another home mortgage.

If you are desperate, my suggestion is that you immediately call the mortgage lender to see whether it's possible to make an arrangement that would benefit both of you. Perhaps instead of foreclosure, you can simply give the lender a deed to your property. (Lenders sometimes prefer to threaten to foreclose, hoping to pressure you into keeping up your payments. Have your attorney look into the possibility of bankruptcy for you. The threat of a personal bankruptcy holding up disposition of a home for months, perhaps years, often brings a reluctant lender around to your way of seeing things.)

FIGURE 20.2
Checklist for When Your House Doesn't Sell

YES NO

☐ ☐ 1. How is the general resale market in your area?

☐ ☐ 2. If it's bad, have you tried reducing your price?

☐ ☐ 3. Why not?

☐ ☐ 4. Do you have a bad location?

☐ ☐ 5. If yes, have you tried reducing your price?

☐ ☐ 6. Why not?

☐ ☐ 7. Have you rechecked comparables lately?

☐ ☐ 8. If your house is priced above market, have you reduced the price?

☐ ☐ 9. Why not?

☐ ☐ 10. Have you asked several agents about the appearance of your home?

☐ ☐ 11. If it shows badly, have you improved it?

☐ ☐ 12. Why not?

☐ ☐ 13. Are you offering seller-financed terms?

☐ ☐ 14. If not, why not?

☐ ☐ 15. Have you considered listing?

☐ ☐ 16. Why not?

☐ ☐ 17. Have you considered leasing?

☐ ☐ 18. What about a lease option?

☐ ☐ 19. If you're desperate, have you considered a deed in lieu of foreclosure?

☐ ☐ 20. Have you talked with an attorney?

Tips on Auctioning Off Your Home

Have you considered holding an auction to sell your home?

It's not the sort of thing that most people think about. Yet, if handled correctly, and if there's enough publicity, you can use the technique to get rid of an otherwise hard-to-sell property. (In some rare cases you can even get above market price for it!)

A home auction is just what it sounds like. You get people to bid on your property until the winning bid buys the home, hopefully at a price you want to sell it for.

Sound simple? It is. On the other hand, there are many pitfalls. Selling a single home at auction can be one of the most difficult auctioneering tasks. Here are the pros and cons. (At the end of this chapter, we'll discuss possible restrictions on holding an auction in your area.)

Why Would I Want to Sell at Auction?

There are basically three reasons to hold an auction:

1. *You want a quick sale.* The entire auction process can take as little time as a few weeks. It's an excellent way to get out of your home, fast.

2. *You have a hard-to-sell home.* Perhaps you've tried to sell FSBO and have been unsuccessful. Maybe you've tried to

sell by listing with an agent, and also have been unsuccessful. Your last, best hope now becomes the auction.

3. *The timing is right.* Home auctions work best in two
kinds of markets: very slow and very hot. In a slow market, people come by hoping to get a steal. In a hot market, people come by because there are few homes in the
housing inventory and they hope to get one.

How Does It Work?

You've probably been to or at least seen an auction. The
usual image most of us have is of a crowd of people sitting in a
room (or under a tent) with an auctioneer at a lectern in front
describing various "lots" for sale and banging down a gavel when
the successful bidder wins.

That's the traditional auction. Indeed, many times auction
companies will handle a home auction in exactly the same way,
if they have a group of homes to dispose of. They will offer a
period of time for viewing the home. They will provide an arena
for the auction. And then a professional auctioneer will sell off
the properties.

That works well when you have many properties to sell. A
kind of fever builds at such times and a skillful auctioneer can often get a better price for the homes than the market may warrant.

However, in your case you only have one home. There's no
real time to build up enthusiasm. So I suggest a "silent" auction.
Here buyers make silent bids for the property during an open auction period. (Bidders can either see other bids as in an open auction, or the bids can be sealed as in a closed auction.) When the
auction period ends, the bids are all opened and the winner gets
the house.

But it's not quite that simple, as we'll see.

What Are the Problems I Will Face?

To pull off a successful auction, you will need to jump a series of hurdles. Figure 21.1 lists of most of them.

FIGURE 21.1
Hurdles to Overcome

1. Handling the paperwork. This includes the auction documents as well as the usual purchase agreement and other documents.

2. Getting publicity. An auction will only work if lots of people know about it. Usually they have to learn of it quickly, just before the auction is held. It's your job to get the word out.

3. Qualifying bidders. You need to qualify bidders, otherwise anyone can make a bid, even the neighborhood cat!

4. Deciding on the auction's form. Do you want an open or a closed auction?

5. Deciding whether to sell "absolute" or hold a reserve. Absolute means that no matter how low the winning bid, you'll still sell the house. Holding a reserve means that there's a minimum price below which you won't go.

6. Handling the actual auction. Someone has to conduct and you know who that's going to be!

7. Closing the sale. What happens if the top bidder can't get a mortgage?

How Do I Handle the Paperwork?

This should be pretty easy, if you've read through this book so far. For the usual work, you can find a real estate agent who can handle the sales agreement and other documentation and hire that person for a fee, which you can negotiate.

There will, however, be some additional paperwork, namely the documentation that spells out the terms of the auction. This needs to be done correctly so you don't get into legal trouble later on (as when there's no defined process for determining who's the winner with two identical bids). A good attorney, hopefully one who's handled auctions before, can be invaluable here. Negotiate a set fee for doing all the paperwork.

> ## CAUTION
>
> Some states restrict the ability of people to hold public auctions. Be sure to have your attorney check into the rules for your state. For example, it could be the case that you'll be unable to hold a public auction without hiring a professional auctioneer, which may or may not prove to be prohibitively expensive.

How Do I Handle the Publicity?

People are much more inclined to want to read about an auction than a simple house for sale. The word *auction* implies getting a bargain, and people are always up for bargains.

Therefore, I suggest you use the usual methods, only emphasize the words "House Auction." Advertise in the local newspapers, put out flyers (where allowed to do so), put a big sign on the property, even consider taking some low-cost spots on the local cable channel. If there's a major thoroughfare nearby, ask (or offer to pay a nominal sum to) a neighbor if you can place an auction sign on his or her lawn for a week. Many people are quite amenable to doing this, although some aren't.

It's critical that you get the word out to as many people as possible. The more who learn of the auction, the more who are likely to bid.

> ## CAUTION
>
> While being sure your advertisements contain enough information to whet the appetite of potential bidders, be sure they also contain enough disclaimers to protect you. Your attorney can help you with this.

How Do I Qualify Buyers?

This is a huge problem. You want as many bidders as possible. On the other hand, you want to be sure that the bidders you get are sincere and can afford the property.

How do you accomplish this?

One method is to have a fee for bidding. The fee need not be large, say only $25, and it can be fully refundable if the bidder is unsuccessful. (Some states prohibit accepting deposits that are not fully refundable.) Nevertheless, asking a person to put up some money up front often shakes out the wheat from the chaff. Only serious bidders will usually apply.

Further, you can insist that to obtain a bidding form (described below) the bidder must show that he or she has a deposit of a certain amount (typically $1,000 to $5,000) ready to give to you. They don't actually give the money to you, just show that they have it, usually in the form of a cashier's check made out to an escrow company. (See below.)

Additionally, you can insist that in order to bid, the bidders provide a preapproval letter from a lender. As we saw in Chapter 14, these are very easy to get and are commonplace today. The letter should state at minimum the size of a mortgage the bidder can qualify for. You can immediately tell if it's big enough.

Of course, there's the matter of the bidder coming up with enough money for the down payment and the closing costs. Usually this is handled at the time of choosing the winning bid. You can give the winning bidder a short period of time (24 to 72 hours) to come up with verification of enough money to close the deal. This is in addition to the deposit already described.

If the winning bidder can't do it, then you move down to the next bidder. (This is why you need expert help in creating your documentation—it must specify exactly what's to happen in this eventuality.)

Should I Sell Open or Closed?

In an open sale, each bidder can see how high the previous bid was. This encourages bidders to move the price up. However, the bidders can also see if there are few to no bids and if they are low. That discourages them from bidding or encourages low-ball bids.

If the sale is closed, the bidders have no idea how many other bids there are or what they are. This encourages people to make bids. However, there is no impetus to beat out other people, hence the bids may be disappointingly low.

Open or closed? There are arguments on both sides and you have to decide which to use in your locale.

Should I Sell Absolute or with Reserve?

For most people, this is an easy call. Put a reserve in, lest you sell your house for too little. Remember, a reserve is a minimum price below which you will not sell. It's only self-protection.

Be aware that if you put a reserve in, you must disclose that you have a reserve to all potential bidders. Most people will just assume that you've put your reserve at or close to market price, hence there's no real steal to be obtained. Thus, putting in a reserve discourages bidding.

On the other hand, advertise that this is an absolute sale and you'll have people coming from all over to bid. Absolute means that the top bid wins, no matter how low it may be. Everyone will want to enter a bid in the hopes of getting something for nothing. You'll get oodles of bids. Unfortunately, most may be very low.

Combining an absolute sale with an open bidding process sometimes results in the highest bids.

CAUTION

Remember, if the sale is absolute, you must sell to the highest bidder, even if that bid is for only $100!

How Do I Handle the Actual Auction? (Silent)

Usually there's an auction time period. It could be a few hours, a day, a few days, or even a few weeks. During the designated period, bidders are allowed to make their bids.

Typically the bid is on a prescribed form that your attorney will give you that is appropriate for your state. Because most auctions are for cash to the seller, it is assumed that the buyer will have enough money for a down payment and will also get a new mortgage. This can be spelled out.

Also, there is usually a provision that the winning bidder must have a deposit (noted above and typically a cashier's check, for a minimum amount, perhaps $1,000 to $5,000) to give to you at the time that winner is announced. This is to cement the sale and is the equivalent of the normal deposit found in any real estate transaction.

If the winning bidder can't immediately produce the cashier's check, the bid is voided and the next highest bidder selected.

Once the winning bidder is announced and produces the appropriate deposit, you conclude the sale by filling out and signing a sales agreement (usually handled by an agent or attorney) in the manner described in Chapter 13.

And you've sold your home! (Hopefully for a high price!)

How Do I Handle the Closing?

The closing is handled in the usual manner described in Chapter 19. The auction process is just used to produce a buyer. Once you have a buyer, everything else proceeds as usual.

The one exception is that you also have backup buyers, all those unsuccessful bidders. This is useful in keeping pressure on the winning bidder to keep things moving along. He or she realizes that if they don't financially perform, you have other buyers waiting in the wings.

> # FACT
>
> Don't count on those other buyers. They may have long since forgotten about the auction or have purchased other properties. They are nice to have to keep the pressure on the winning bidder, but are seldom there if you actually need to use them.

What about State Restrictions?

Each state handles auctions a little differently. Some are very strict and require that the process be handled by a licensed professional. Others are more laid back and don't seem to care very much. Most, however, are quite specific about saying you must reveal whether the auction is absolute or reserve.

Before conducting your auction, it is important that you check with a professional in your state to be sure you're in compliance with all local laws.

Can I Really Do It?

You certainly can give it a try. Many people have quickly and profitably sold their homes using auctions. On the other hand, far, far more people have handled their sales in the more conventional manner.

Index